GHOSTS-
MURDER-MAYHEM:
A CHRONICLE OF SANTA FE

Lies, Legends, Facts, Tall Tales and Useless Information

GHOSTS-MURDER-MAYHEM:
A CHRONICLE OF SANTA FE

Lies, Legends, Facts, Tall Tales and Useless Information

By
Allan Pacheco

SUNSTONE PRESS

SANTA FE

Sunstone books may be purchased for educational, business, or sales promotional use. For information please write: Special Markets Department, Sunstone Press, P.O. Box 2321, Santa Fe, New Mexico 87504-2321.

Library of Congress Cataloging-in-Publication Data:

Pacheco, Allan, 1961-
    Ghosts-murder-mayhem, a chronicle of Santa Fe : lies, legends, facts, tall tales, and useless information / by Allan Pacheco.
        p. cm.
    Includes bibliographical references.
    ISBN 0-86534-410-8 (softcover)
1. Santa Fe (N.M.)—History—Anecdotes. 2. Santa Fe (N.M.)—Social life and customs—Anecdotes. 3. Santa Fe (N.M.)—Biography—Anecdotes. 4. Crime—New Mexico—Santa Fe—History—Anecdotes. 5. Ghosts—New Mexico—Santa Fe—Anecdotes. 6. Legends—New Mexico—Santa Fe. 7. Tall tales—New Mexico—Santa Fe. 8. Folklore—New Mexico—Santa Fe. I. Title.

F804.S257P33 2004
978.9'56—dc22

                                    2004015240

Published in

WWW.SUNSTONEPRESS.COM
SUNSTONE PRESS / POST OFFICE BOX 2321 / SANTA FE, NM 87504-2321 /USA
(505) 988-4418 / ORDERS ONLY (800) 243-5644 / FAX (505) 988-1025

A special thanks to those who made this book happen:

Orlando, Don, Waco, Lily, Christy, Adelo, Jim, and Guadalupe.

We also thank the various unknown artists and photographers
whose images have inspired and served as strong references
for the stylized drawings of Dean Howell

Special acknowledgment goes to Santa Fe artist Dean Howell
for his original drawings plus his stylized interpretations of
historical images which have captured the spirit of this book.

CONTENTS

1

GHOSTS:
THE UNEXPLAINED,
HOAX AND MIRACLES

A SPIRIT IN SANTA FE

The Staab House at 330 East Palace Avenue, which is now La Posada resort, is home to the ghost of Julia Schuster Staab. On May 14, 1896, at 10:30 P.M., in what is now room 100, Julia died in her bedroom at the age of fifty-two. Some accounts have her being younger. Julia was a petite woman with large dark eyes, fair skin, and shoulder length hair. A portrait of Julia hangs in room 100. Her beauty is striking. Some old Santa Feans claim that the painting is of Julia's daughter who was a lookalike of her mother; others say it's a portrait of Julia's niece. Be it a facsimile through her daughter or niece, one has to agree that Mrs. Staab was alluring and stylish. Tragically, Julia's spirit has not found peace and she haunts La Posada.

Guests who have stayed in room 100 have reported hearing footsteps and feeling cold streams of air even though the windows are closed. Other happenings in this room include lights unexplainably being turned on or off and the sensation of being watched.

Why does Julia's ghost haunt La Posada? The answer may lie in the unhappy life that Julia had at the Staab House. Julia was the German born wife of wealthy Abraham Staab.

Abraham was born in 1839 in Lüdge, Germany. He made his wealth in America by furnishing southwest Union garrisons with supplies during territorial and Civil War days. Abraham returned to Germany and married Julia in a Jewish ceremony in 1865. The duo then moved to Santa Fe. Abraham had the Staab House built in 1870; different sources have different dates.

The Staab House of the 1880s was known as the Staab mansion. Abraham furnished his residence with the richest of items. Abraham was a possessor of exquisite things and sadly Julia became one of his possessions.

Julia had many roles in her marriage and each role became worse than the last. At first Julia was the arm candy that Abraham showed off while he strolled Santa Fe. Later Julia's role became that of Abraham's entertaining, gracious, socialite wife. Contrariwise, Julia was not a typical ornamental wife; she was kind and her contemporaries spoke highly of her.

Legend has it, as Abraham became wealthier, he became promiscuous and controlling towards Julia. Over a short amount of time, Abraham had turned the Staab House into Julia's prison. She was sequestered away and forced into becoming Abraham's baby machine.

Julia gave birth to five children and had many premature stillbirths. Some accounts say Julia had eight miscarriages and more children. Whatever the number, Julia was treated as an automaton, without feelings. One of Julia's sons died at an early age. These tragedies coupled with Abraham's unfaithfulness and his tyrannical ways made

Julia's hair turn prematurely gray. Slowly Julia lost her physical and mental health.

In 1891, Abraham announced that Julia had become ill and would be tended to, in what is now room 100. Nobody saw Julia during the last five years of her life, and, according to Abraham, Julia remained very ill until her death in 1896.

After Julia's death many rumors circulated in Santa Fe about what caused her demise. One hearsay was that Julia had been driven insane by her husband's physical and mental abuse. She died as a captive in her bedroom in the throws of crazed emotion.

Another rumor was that Julia died of a broken heart due to Abraham's mistreatment of her. Julia, feeling unloved and constantly cheated upon, slipped into a deep melancholy; lacking the will to live, she passed on.

Another whisper is that Abraham murdered Julia or had somebody murder her on the night of May 14, 1896. Poison or strangulation were some of the wild theories.

In 1913, Abraham died and the Staab House was sold and resold and in 1936 it became a hotel-resort. Over the years the old Staab property has been expanded upon and buildings have been added. La Posada uses the Staab House as its main building. The old mansion houses a restaurant, guest rooms, and a lounge.

Once the Staab House became a hotel, the ghost of Julia started making appearances in the main building in different forms. When Julia's shade is seen in full silhouette, the spirit wears a red Victorian dress and hat. The emotion that this apparition gives off is that of curiosity or of sadness, slowness, and being deep in thought.

This vision of Julia in the long Victorian dress manifests itself on the stairwell area that leads to room 100 (originally room 256 until a remodeling in 1998-1999). Infrequently, Julia is seen in this guise in the old outside garden area and in the bureau mirror that stands in the corner of room 100.

When Julia is seen as a fast white shadowy blur it is reported that a cold gust of wind usually follows. This manifestation of Julia is occasionally observed in the lounge area of the hotel.

Julia blows past employees and guests, trays fall over, drinks are spilled, and the outside doors to the inner courtyard are violently opened. The feeling one gets from this version of Julia is that of anger and judgment.

La Posada was remodeled during the late 1990s and many bizarre things occurred. Contemporary lore states that construction workers returning in the morning to work on room 100 found their tools strewn about. The night before, the workers had neatly put their tools away and had locked the room's doors as a precaution against theft.

More strange things happened as room 100 was revamped. The tools were now left alone but the electric extension cords would be found knotted up in the morning. There was no explanation for this. The workers had locked the room behind them and had left their cords untangled.

As remodeling moved from the bedroom to the bathroom of room 100, stranger things occurred. New porcelain bathroom fixtures inexplicably cracked after installation. In one instance a brand new toilet fell to pieces overnight and the water from it flooded parts of the Staab House.

The creepiest story attributed to Julia was that construction workers were harassed by occasional prank rings that came from the telephone in room 100. The phone line to room 100 had been disconnected during the remodeling. The switchboard operator also received calls from room 100. When the phone was answered there was dead silence.

Santa Fe lore asserts that occasionally there was heard over the line, mumbled unintelligible, distant words that were masked by a strange static-like sound. Perhaps the words were German or Yiddish.

Julia's ghost obviously did not like the reconstruction of the Staab House, much less her room.

The refurbishing of the Staab House unfortunately did not release Julia's spirit. Julia's appearances are so common at La Posada that her manifestations are now rarely reported being that it's so familiar.

Nonetheless, one question remains. Why does Julia's spirit linger at the Staab House? Is the answer to this query found in how Julia died?

Perhaps in her terrible passing, be it insanity or melancholy, Julia did not realize that she was dead. Or was she murdered and her ghost is some type of vengeance?

Julia was buried at the Fairview Cemetery which is located at the crossroads of Cerrillos and Cordova roads. Is there an answer as to why Julia haunts La Posada, and can that answer be found at her grave site or at La Posada?

If you're brave and have sensitivity, spend a night in room 100. Maybe you can find out why Julia's spirit haunts the resort. Many people have tried to stay the night in Julia's old bedchamber. Some have made it, others have become so afraid that they've had to check out early or demand another room. Santa Fe lore has it that actor/singer Kris Kristofferson tried a night in room 100 but didn't make it. Think you can? Good luck! [1]

Staab House, La Posada Resort

THE LEGEND
OF SCHOOL BOY DEAD
AND THE WOMAN IN BLACK

The PERA (Public Employees Retirement Administration) building was constructed in 1966 and is located at 1120 Paseo de Peralta. It is haunted by a ghost that appears as a woman dressed in black. Prior to 1966, the property included athletic fields and buildings that belonged to St. Michael's High School.

A walled graveyard was also on the grounds. It was supposedly in use until the late 1800s. Records are not clear as to when the cemetery was first and last used.

During the mid-1960s as the PERA building was being constructed, the old school buildings were knocked down and the graveyard was dug up. Legend has it that not all the burial ground was unearthed and a major portion of the old cemetery was graded flat and then paved over. This surfaced area is now the PERA building's parking lot.

It is alleged that the old walled graveyard had always been haunted by spirits. Some old-timers say it was haunted by just one ghost that appeared in the guise of a woman garbed in black.

After the PERA building's completion, janitors who worked nights in the building reported they heard footsteps walking down empty hallways. In the early 1970s, an apparition described as a lady dressed in black was seen disappearing into walls or vanishing while walking down deserted corridors.

Catholic Brother, Steve Armenta, who taught at the new St. Michael's High School, shed some light on the Lady in Black legend. In the 1800s, St. Michael's was an institute of renown. Wealthy parents from all over the Southwest and Mexico sent their teenage sons to St. Michael's as boarding students.

Tragically, in 1867 a dormitory's water supply became contaminated with disease, perhaps cholera. Two of the boarding students died from drinking the bad water. The two students were buried in the cemetery that now lies beneath the PERA building's parking lot.

Doña Maria Pena de Sanchez and her husband came to Santa Fe from Colorado when word reached them about their son's death. Upon arriving, the Sanchezes learned that their son and the other deceased student had been buried and Catholic Mass had already been conducted.

Doña Maria's grief was compounded when the graveyard officials along with the St. Michael's staff could not identify which of the new graves was her son's. After paying his respects, Mr. Sanchez returned to Colorado to manage his ranch.

Doña Maria decided to stay in Santa Fe and walked daily to the grave site and prayed a rosary alternating between the graves that could contain her boy's body. As the years passed, Doña Maria continued her pilgrimage to the graveyard. Eventually this heartbroken parent died.

It seems that even in death Doña Maria continues to go to the grave sites that are now somewhere in the parking lot. This could explain why janitors or employees occasionally see a specter dressed in black walk down halls and pass through walls. Is that specter Doña Maria, or is it the shadow of some other troubled spirit? [2]

RUN FOR YOUR LIFE!

Santa Fe's "La Llorona," which means "The Crying Woman," is not to be confused with the Aztec specter who shares the same name. Santa Fe's La Llorona has no tie-in with that ghost.

The Aztec La Llorona, who was heard in Mexico City during the reign of Emperor Montezuma II, was an apparition who cried out at night. This shadow gave warning that the Aztec Empire was about to be toppled by light-skinned invaders from the East.

Through La Llorona's sobs the Aztecs heard vague predictions: "Children, where can we hide? I fear what is going to happen to us." This prophesying banshee was correct, for light-skinned Spanish Conquistadors led by Captain Cortez did destroy the Aztec Empire and they did come from across the sea from the East.

Santa Fe's La Llorona legend asserts that during Spanish Colonial days there was a woman named Luisa de Olveros, or Maria. Her last name varies to such a great degree that it has become lost to history.

Maria's lover was a man of the Spanish nobility, and he would not marry her on the excuse that she had two children out of wedlock.

In a fit of evil insanity, Maria drowned her two children and then went to the nobleman lover who rejected her. In the deepest of sorrow, Maria went back to the ditch or river bank where she had killed her children and committed suicide. Her ghost, La Llorona, now travels the waterways and dry gully beds of the Santa Fe area searching and crying for her two youngsters she murdered.

During the 1940s through 1950s La Llorona was reported to be roaming the Acequia Madre area of Santa Fe. "Acequia Madre" means "Mother Ditch." La Llorona has been heard as far west as Albuquerque and as far north as Taos. From 1969 to 1971, a rash of sightings or hearings that concerned La Llorona were reported all over Santa Fe. Since that time, the reports of seeing or hearing La Llorona have become sparse.

Some quipsters with a wink of an eye say that, "La Llorona is now somewhere in Texas, frightening Texicans as she follows streams and rivers to the Gulf of Mexico." Maybe they are right, and then again, maybe La Llorona is still in the Santa Fe area.

La Llorona is a very dangerous ghost who will kill adults or children. Lore has it that La Llorona prefers to take her victims away with her rather than kill them on the spot. These victims are never seen again.

People who have heard La Llorona say the voice comes from many different areas of a river or gully and it is near impossible to track down the source of the crying woman. The few who have seen the ghost claim that at a distance La Llorona is a very beautiful woman, but up close La Llorona changes into a horrible ravaged hag.

Over the years there have been a few mysterious cases where a child or adult is reported missing in the Santa Fe area and no clues are found. The authorities claim these puzzling incidents are just well covered-up murders and time will reveal who did it and where the body is.

Some weird beard Santa Feans profess that the missing person was abducted by aliens and others say it was La Llorona. For all of that, in some of these missing people cases, the body has never been recovered and nobody has been charged with the crime.

Is there a La Llorona and was there a woman who drowned her children in the Colonial days?

Lore has it that La Llorona's drowned children were buried in the cemetery that is underneath the PERA building at 1120 Paseo De Peralta. La Llorona was supposedly buried in a deep unmarked grave alongside the Santa Fe River. Until the early 1800s, the Santa Fe River was not a dried out creek but a torrent that flowed to the Rio Grande River.

Texarkana has the creature of Boggy Creek, the Pine Barrens has the Jersey Devil, and Santa Fe has La Llorona, the most dangerous of all phantoms. If you ever hear or see this apparition, make tracks in the opposite direction. This banshee according to some Santa Feans is legit and lethal. As the Robot would say in the television series, *Lost In Space*, "Danger, danger, Will Robinson!" [3]

A SINISTER EVIL NIGHT

Witch lore tells of Juana Chavez who lived in Nambe which is north of Santa Fe. Chavez was a "Bruja," which means an evil, powerful sorceress. Chavez's powers enabled her to cast spells that caused accidents, sickness, and lightning strikes. This story is hard to pinpoint. Some say this witch lived during Spanish Colonial times. Others declare it occurred during Santa Fe's "Wild West" days. In any case, the story has been passed on from generation to generation.

Chavez's black magic was so powerful her spells could kill people over a time span of a few days. This bruja's incantations were discharged by way of chants, voodoo dolls, or by hitting the bottom of her fist into the palm of her other hand.

The people of Nambe became fed up with Juana Chavez's deeds. The villagers gathered together and marched on her house. What death or catastrophe mobilized the villagers of Nambe to act is not clear.

The townspeople of Nambe locked Chavez into her house and fired it, whereupon Chavez was burned to death. After the fire had gone out, the citizens of Nambe found evil-looking dolls that had been hidden in the foundation of Chavez's house. Little did the Nambe villagers know that these evil dolls had hidden themselves in the house's substructure.

The villagers gathered the unscorched effigies and stacked them into a pyre. As the big mound of wicked-looking dolls was about to be ignited, they animated. The villainous small effigies ran about trying to escape the torches of the Nambe villagers. All night long the ugly dolls were chased down and set on fire.

The story of Juana Chavez is likely based on embellished facts, because there are factual cases of witches in Nambe having been put to death. It's of note that New Mexico's history is filled with tales of witches, spells, and just comeuppance. In 1675, four witches were hanged and numerous others were whipped. During the 1880s, two witches were clubbed to death. In 1940, Avelino Espinoza was arrested for being a witch. He supposedly attacked people while not in human form. As for Juana Chavez's dolls, some forms of black magic use inanimate figures that resemble humans, animals, or demons. Did the dolls come to life? Anything is possible in the "Twilight Zone" area of northern Santa Fe County. [4]

THE TEN TON STORY!

Orson Wells' 1938 War of the Worlds broadcast is forever remembered as "The Night that Panicked America." In spite of that, Orson and his Mercury Theater radio show have to take a back seat to the "Ten Ton Story" that hoaxed all of Santa Fe in 1973.

On Tuesday, August 7, 1973, around 6:30 P.M., the first words of the calamity were heard. CB operators between Santa Fe and Albuquerque heard the hysterical screams of Larry over a CB radio channel.

Larry was a six-year-old boy who was trapped with the corpse of his father inside the cab of an overturned pickup truck. Larry claimed that his father had crashed off a dirt road and into a gully. Larry repeatedly panicked as he yelled for help when the radio frequency would fade on him.

Complicating matters was that Larry in his hysteria would switch from channel to channel as he screamed into the microphone for help.

Through his sobs Larry admitted that he knew nothing of how the CB radio worked.

People who listened to Larry found out that the boy did not have any food or water and had no idea what part of New Mexico he was in. The radio signal faded in and out due to atmospherics, and nobody could guess how much life Larry's CB battery had in it.

The night of August 7, and the early morning of August 8, was a very strange evening for ionospherics. Radio operators from California to England affirmed that they heard the faint pleas and screams from Larry due to the radio skip that occurred that evening.

New Mexico Search and Rescue as well as the local police departments were able to vector onto Larry's CB signal. Larry's signal was thought to be coming from an area that stretched from Albuquerque to Santa Fe.

By the morning of August 8, the Santa Fe Police, the Albuquerque Police, the State Police, as well as the local search and rescue teams began to hunt for Larry. The search was badly coordinated and badly led. Thousands of volunteers left their jobs to look for Larry, but these searchers were not instructed or guided as to what territory to cover.

Linda King, who lived in Albuquerque and went by the CB name of "Blue Eyes," was able to get more information from Larry than anybody else who was officially part of the police search. "Blue Eyes" was just an ordinary civilian who stayed up day and night trying to get Larry to calm down and give the search teams a landmark to sight. Linda was an unsung hero.

Linda King and other CB hobbyists were able to get Larry to give out his last name, Cortesi. Through the garble of radio static it was found out that Larry's father's name was David.

Larry was now growing weaker and his CB signal was fading. Compounding Larry's ordeal was that the day's temperatures were in the 80s and 90s.

Prayer groups got together and addressed the Lord. Psychics called the police departments and gave their predictions of where Larry would be found.

Local television stations covered the search for Larry with broadcast bulletins and on-the-spot mini cams. At times the media ballyhoo around the Larry search resembled the Billy Wilder film, *Ace In the Hole*, filmed in New Mexico in 1951. *Ace In The Hole* concerned itself with the media hype that surrounded the rescue attempt of a man who was trapped in a New Mexico mine shaft cave-in. In the movie the authorities blundered in their rescue attempt to save the trapped man.

On the night of August 8, Larry reported with screams over the CB that a propeller airplane had flown by his overturned, crashed truck. Larry could see the lights and hear the engine of the plane, but no one could confirm any such flight.

The search now centered from Tijeras, which is outside of Albuquerque, to the outskirts of Santa Fe. The searchers found abandoned houses, junked or stolen vehicles, and all types of debris. The overturned truck was not found.

Late Friday night, on August 10th, the search went out of control. By the morning of August 11th, the search was as organized as a riot. Volunteers swarmed the well traveled dirt roads west of Santa Fe with their CBs on. The air waves were jammed with voices calling for Larry.

Larry's weak voice was drowned out by the constant chatter of the searchers. Some adults and children got into the act and mimicked Larry's voice over their own base stations or portable CBs. Searchers were tricked and spent precious time tracking down bogus signal locations.

Larry's voice finally faded away, but the search went on until Sunday night of August 12th. The end result was that nobody had reported a boy by the name of Larry missing and the searchers had not found an overturned pickup.

The conclusion was that Larry had been a sick adult who had carried out the biggest hoax since Orson Wells' radio broadcast.

The frightening thing about this hoaxer is that he has kept his secret. Nobody has admitted that he was Larry, in 1973. Then again, I hope it was a hoax. [5]

Search and Rescue Microphone

THE DEVIL'S BURNING HAND
AND THE
CASE OF DON DIABLO

This is a tall story if there ever was one, but the oldsters of Santa Fe claim that it happened back in the late 1940s at the G.E.O. (George King Bar) that was then located at 110 Galisteo.

Supposedly, late one Fiesta night a group of men and women were drinking and arguing around a table that was near the bar door. The group quarreled about souls and evil, what is real and what does not exist.

Outside the bar, a lightning storm lit up the evening sky of Santa Fe. The squabblers became more emotional with their arguments about whether the Devil exists or not. One of the nonbelievers promised a believer a case of Don Diablo Tequila if he could prove that the Devil existed. The non-believer thought he had laid down a bet that would never be collected upon.

Soon after the challenge, a tall, well-dressed, handsome man with a thin mustache, trimmed beard, and a receding hairline that exposed his bony cranium came into the bar. The handsome man looked around at the patrons with his small dark eyes.

The arguing table quieted as the well-groomed man, with a stiff gait, walked toward the quarrelsome table. The man's boots made a clop, clop kind of sound as he walked.

Quick whispers went through the quibbling group. Could this be Beelzebub himself? This was followed by hand signals that signify the sign of the cross. The man who had bet the case of Don Diablo Tequila gulped and shrugged off the approaching man as just another tourist in town for the Fiesta.

The stranger now stood next to the man who bet the case of tequila and roared out the word, "Proof!" With a terrible laugh, the well-dressed man stepped toward the front door and put his hand against the door, burning a hand print into the wood.

A lightning bolt then struck an area near the bar causing the cantina to shake. The handsome stranger then turned into a red devil as he disappeared into a cloud of putrid phosphorous smoke.

The people at the table and the other revelers were dumbfounded. They had just seen the Devil. The man who had said that there was no such thing ended up buying a case of Don Diablo Tequila for the man he issued the bet against.

Supposedly the hand print of the Devil was on the door of the G.E.O. King Bar until the business was closed down and the building remodeled in the early 1960s. Another tall Santa Fe tale, or a legend with a lot of truth?

BROTHER CAN YOU
SPARE A DIME?

The La Fonda Hotel, at 100 East San Francisco, is said to be haunted by the ghost of a businessman from the 1800s. La Fonda was known by many names in the 1800s, such as: The Exchange, The American Fonda, The U.S. Hotel, and The Fonda.

During the 1800s, La Fonda had the reputation as the most elegant hotel in the Southwest. It served fine foods, had billiards, liquor, gambling, and clean accommodations. In the central area of La Fonda there used to be an open gardened courtyard with a well. Today that area is the Plazuela Restaurant.

According to legend, a businessman spent a day and evening at La Fonda drinking and gambling. By the end of the evening the nameless man had lost all his money and was heavily in debt. Desperate over his actions, the unlucky gambler in a crazed state ran into the inner courtyard and committed suicide by jumping into the well.

Now and then a specter of a man in clothing from the 1800s is supposedly seen running across the Plazuela Restaurant. The specter disappears as he jumps into the ground where the old well used to be. Furthermore, maintenance men have seen this specter in the bowels of the hotel. This is followed by storage areas being found topsy turvy. As Ripley would say, "Believe it or not." [6]

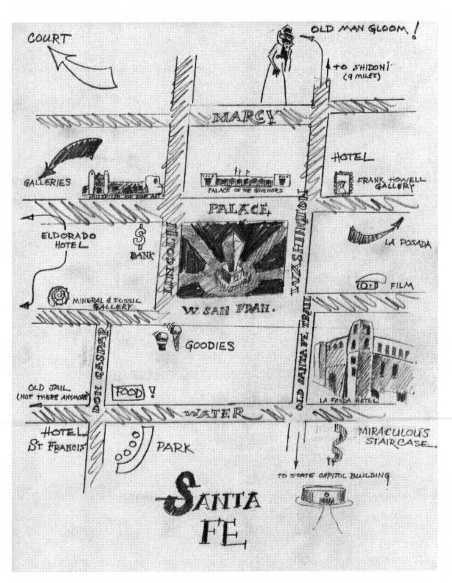

Downtown Santa Fe

MERCY!

Night watchmen and janitors at the Palace of the Governors, which is on the north side of the Plaza, claim to have seen a specter and heard pleas coming from rooms inside this huge building.

The Palace of the Governors is a logical spot for a haunting. During the Indian revolt of August 1680, the royal residence was a fortress that housed over a thousand Spaniards. These Spanish settlers along with Conquistadors battled the Indian armies that tried to storm the building.

In one battle alone over three hundred Indian warriors were killed in the Plaza in hand-to-hand combat. It's safe to presume that unknown numbers of Indians and Spaniards died atop, inside, and outside the Palace of the Governors during the revolt.

Are those laments and pleas for mercy coming from a Spaniard or an Indian who was wounded in battle and later succumbed to his injuries while inside the stately residence? Or is the mumbled voice that asks for mercy the ghost of one of the eight Spaniards who were held as prisoners at the Palace of the Governors in 1643?

The eight Spanish prisoners of 1643 were tried and found guilty of conspiracy and murder. Their victim was Luis de Rosas who was the ex-governor of New Mexico. Rosas was stabbed to death due to his affair with a married woman. However, many of the conspirators who were involved in the murder took part in it because of a political vendetta. On July 21, 1643, the eight Spaniards were decapitated on the Plaza.

No one knows for sure who or what haunts the Palace of the Governors, but it very well could be of these men who lost their heads. Or do these moans and cries belong to a prisoner from another age who was incarcerated inside the old fortress? Then again, are these noises the result of creaking wood and is the specter the result of a fertile imagination? [7]

EVIL AT THE EDGE OF TOWN?

South of Santa Fe off Interstate 25 is the KOA campground. Legend has it that this bivouac is haunted.

According to J. Buckner of California, he and his family stayed at this campground and they were frightened by evil dreams and strange noises. Buckner dreamt that his cabin was visited by a large group of uninvited people who acted like zombies.

These soulless humans, after crowding into the cabin, soon started losing their body parts. Arms and legs fell off these zombies and blood spilled out onto the cabin's floor. After that nightmare of vacant-eyed humans, Buckner packed up his family and left.

Supposedly, a member of the Heaven's Gate cult stayed at this bivouac ages ago. Lore has it, that he received his mail there and was visited by other cult members. Tragically, in 1997 thirty-nine members of the cult committed suicide in Rancho Santa Fe, California, when the Hale Bopp comet appeared. Autopsies on the corpses found that many cult members had been castrated years before. Is there any link between the cult and the nightmare, or is it all pure rubbish? [8]

THE CANNIBAL
WITCHES OF NAMBE

In 1854, Luis Romero and Antonio Tafolla were charged with practicing Black Magic, abduction, murder, and cannibalism in Nambe, which is located in Santa Fe County.

The two witches were found guilty of satanic deeds and lead away from Nambe. It was not clear how many miles the two witches were marched. What is indisputable is that after a long trek the two witches were forced to sit next to each other and then they were executed by a shotgun blast to the head. The four-man execution squad had been appointed by the Nambe Governor to act as provost officers.

Santa Fe, which is south of Nambe, had been under Spanish or Mexican rule since the city's founding in 1610. Due to the Mexican-American War, Santa Fe was occupied by American troops in 1846 and governed by military law. In 1848, Santa Fe became officially part of the United States as New Mexico was annexed into the Union as a territory.

This meant that Santa Fe would now be governed by the territorial court, which is comparable to today's district court system. In March of 1854, Chief Justice Grafton Baker presided over the Territorial Court which was held at the Palace of the Governors.

Under previous Spanish and Mexican rule, witchcraft was punished by death. Now that Santa Fe and the surrounding territory were under American Constitutional law, Santa Feans were puzzled by how the new American legal system would rule when it concerned itself with witchery.

The case of the killing of the two witches was on Baker's docket. The judge had to rule if the four men who had killed the two suspected witches should be prosecuted for murder. Or should the court stand on old Spanish and Mexican laws that stated that killing a witch was justifiable homicide? If Baker went with the old laws, then he would be admitting that witchcraft is a fact, and become a laughing stock in eastern U.S. law societies.

Baker went over the facts of the case; Romero and Tafolla were admitted witches. They had been charged by the Nambe Governor as being sorcerers who cast evil spells. Supposedly the bones of children were found in their house. Thus, the authorities concluded that the two witches had abducted, killed, and eaten children.

Chief Justice Baker understood that Santa Fe under Spanish and Mexican sovereignty had been governed by the decrees of the Inquisition. Witchcraft and the fight between good and evil were accepted as fact by many Santa Feans.

Baker ruled in the affirmative in an odd way and got himself out of having to answer the messy questions: does witchcraft exist and should the territory prosecute the four men who killed the two witches?

Baker claimed that the venue of the executions was not clear, and that nobody could determine if the killings had taken place in Santa Fe County or in Rio Arriba County. On this technicality, Judge Baker closed the case and nothing more was heard.

Santa Feans and the rest of the surrounding territory read between the lines of the judgment. Baker's ruling meant that nothing much had changed as far as how one can defend oneself against evil. Santa Feans thought *viva los Americanos*, they see the world the way we do. [9]

EL WRONGO.
HERE IS THE TRUTH!

One of Santa Fe's tall tales has it that the Coronado building at 141 East Palace Avenue used to be the old Territorial Court House and Territorial Jail. During Santa Fe's "Wild West" days, trial audiences would sometimes become impatient. Once the judge or jury had sentenced a man to death, he was hung on the spot.

The convicted man was hustled out of the courtroom and hung from the large tree that stands outside the Coronado building. Occasionally, one can see the shadow of a hanged man or noose on the front wall of the Coronado Building when the moon is full.

A nice witchy yarn, but only part of the story is true. The Coronado Building was the Territorial Court House, but it was never a jail. Likewise, research has not revealed that any man was ever lynched at that tree outside the building.

Furthermore, Santa Fe's Jail was located at what is now a parking lot at 121 Sandoval Street. At this location provincial authorities conducted public executions by hanging.

As for the Coronado Building, all types of trials were held at this structure. The most infamous was the Borrego y Gonzales murder trial. That story is covered in this book under, "Legitimate Hatred." [10]

The Old Santa Fe Jail and Gallows

THE NAKED HALF TRUTHS– JUMBLED LORE–MIXED UP STORIES THAT ARE PROBABLY BOGUS

The Oldest House, at 215 East De Vargas Street, is home to an interesting ghost story that has been mated to another confused Santa Fe fable. The first story gives no names or dates but asserts that in Spanish Colonial times, two witches lived at the Oldest House.

During this time, two young Santa Fe men courted the same young woman. Although very flattered, the young woman could not choose between her suitors. Unaware of each other's scheme, both love-struck beaus clandestinely visited the witches at the Oldest House and both bought love potions or spells from the sorceresses.

Both suitors were told at the time of purchase that whoever beheld the young woman first and used the spell first would win the damsel's heart. Accordingly, there would be no refunds on this magic. Once the spell was cast or done, there would be no recourse. It would be a fait accompli.

The elixir worked and the woman fell in love with one of the young men. Both families of the new couple agreed to the union and a marriage was planned. The young man who was not chosen became insane with rage and walked into the Oldest House and confronted the two witches.

The young man demanded another potion and satisfaction, but none was forthcoming. With yells and curses the slighted young man attacked the two witches with his fists. The witches grabbed their butcher knives and stabbed the young man to death.

The two witches then decapitated the corpse of the young man, and the head was desecrated and cursed. Legend has it that the severed head was either thrown out into the street in front of the Oldest House or the head was never found and the corpse was buried headless.

It is alleged that the young man's decapitated head is seen rolling down the streets near the Oldest House on stormy nights. This tale ties into the story of a headless horseman who is seen infrequently galloping down Alto Street and then onto the banks of the Santa Fe River.

Is this headless horseman the ghost of the young man who was decapitated by the two witches? Supposedly the Boy's Club off of Alto Street is haunted by an entity, possibly this headless man. The Club's showers and lights are turned on when the building is deserted.

The Alto Street area where this headless horseman gallops does have some house dating back to the Spanish Colonial days. Is one of these old houses on Alto Street the home of the young man who was murdered by the two witches? Or did this decapitated young man once live on the property that now houses the Boy's Club?

Or are these stories, the headless horseman, the club, and the Oldest House decapitation balderdash? [11]

Duendes are ugly, ghostly, dwarves who steal from anybody they come in contact with. To some Santa Feans, mainly Mexican immigrants new to the United States, Duendes are not a myth but a fact.

Duendes came to Spain from Italy during the days of the Roman Empire. From Spain, Duendes came to the New World with the Conquistadors. Wherever the Spaniards settled, from Mexico to Guam, tales of thieving Duendes are found.

Lore has it that Duendes live outside Santa Fe. At midnight, during their nocturnal banquets, these evil beings relish showing off their stolen goods to each other. Duendes use these stolen objects in order to gain amorous favors from beautiful but immoral women.

Irish Leprechaun and Mexican Duende lore are somewhat similar in that if you appease these creatures they will rarely bother your house. It is alleged that if you leave a goat or a bottle of alcohol out for a Duende, the animal or bottle will disappear and the ghostly dwarf will make peace with you. Religious medals or icons also keep Duendes away from one's heirlooms or tools.

Duendes do not like strong winds, so if it's a blustery day you are safe from their irksome thieving ways. Only in Santa Fe will one hear of stories of magical Mexican dwarves running amuck. The long and short of it: sounds like a fictitious imported Mexican fable.

The Grant Corner Inn at 122 Grant Avenue is professed to be haunted by the ghosts of the Robinson family. Santa Fe lore states that a caretaker once witnessed lights going off and on inside the building, noises were heard, and the odor of rotting meat emanated from the wood and brick structure.

The Grant Corner Inn was built in 1905. In 1982, it was converted into a bed and breakfast. Between the dates of 1905 and 1982, the Grant Corner Inn property was used as a residence, a boarding house, and business offices.

The strange occurrences at the Grant Corner Inn have only happened from the 1980s onward. So is the Grant Corner Inn haunted? Or are these stories puffery and the book *The Amityville Horror* was being used as a template for this tale?

The facts and foggy myths concerning the Grant Corner Inn are these. The building's first owner was the Winson family, some sources say the Windsor family. The next owner/resident was Ada Moore, who was the wife of a minister in charge of the First Presbyterian Church at 208 Grant Avenue, which is down the street from the Inn. The minister's first name has been lost in the midst of history.

Ada's minister husband died and years later she married postal worker and mailman Arthur Robinson. Ada and Arthur Robinson lived on the Grant Corner Inn property until their deaths, in 1945 and 1956. Another Santa Fe fable has it that an adult daughter lived in the house until her death in an auto accident in the 1970s. The date like the names are not exact, so one wonders about the authenticity of this haunting.

The Robinsons led a checkered American life. Ada Robinson gave piano lessons and sold the *Denver Post* newspaper. Arthur Robinson was fired from the post office for embezzlement and did some time behind bars for his crime.

Later on, Arthur became Santa Fe's Justice of the Peace and married many people at his residence, which is now Grant Corner Inn. Lore has it that Arthur was known as a tightwad and a grocery store thief. Near the end of his life, he was an invalid and confined to a wheelchair.

So how do these people figure into any ghostly hauntings? There were no murders at the Grant Corner Inn. Did Ada, Arthur, and the adult daughter become cursed by doing some type of secret evil and now they are back at their old residence?

It is of interest that the 1931 murder of Angelina Jaramillo, which is covered in this book under "THE OX BOW INCIDENT OF SANTA FE" happened only a hundred yards away from the Grant Corner Inn. Are you convinced that the Grant Corner Inn is haunted, or is this building just occasionally visited by a manifestation? [12]

The store at 123 West San Francisco is supposedly haunted by a ghost who lives on its upper floors. Records show that the property at 123 West San Francisco was home to the Paris Movie Theater in the 1920s. The theater was sold, refurbished, and renamed the El Paseo in the 1960s.

The El Paseo was renown for having one of the finest big screens in the southwest. The theater was closed in the 1970s and the building later became a disco. During this time sightings of a phantom in the galleria were nil. However, many people were gunned down on the streets that border this building during Santa Fe's six-shooter days. Perhaps there is some merit to this tale, and previous encounters with this ghost were simply not reported.

The Eldorado Hotel at 309 West San Francisco is said to be haunted by two ghosts. The only incident that would signify this structure is haunted would be the death of a construction worker who was killed during the building of the hotel. In 1985, David Gurule was crushed to death when a cement slab fell on him.

Contrarily, through the 1980s and 1990s there were no reports of hauntings at the Eldorado. Only recently have stories of ghosts at the Eldorado been bandied about.

The first Eldorado story states that the apparition of artist Georgia O'Keeffe sleeps on a bed in a top floor suite on the eastern side of the building. O'Keeffe's spirit supposedly leaves an indentation on the bed. When O'Keeffe's ghost is awake, she looks out from her hotel bedroom window onto her museum below. The story sounds a little thin, doesn't it?

The other Eldorado story states that the bar is haunted. Supposedly the bar was closed down one night and left in pristine shape. The next morning the hotel staff found the bar in disarray, bottles had been emptied and broken, glasses were strewn about. Furthermore, a couple of three-foot Kachina dolls that were used to decorate the lounge were missing.

The ransacked bar area and the missing Kachinas is blamed on a ghost. Is it possible that a disgruntled employee and his friends late one night helped themselves to booze and pilfered some Kachina dolls?

Should the Eldorado ghost stories be gonged? As compared to other Santa Fe ghost stories, they are very weak. Where is Chuck Barris and the gong mallet?

Some Santa Feans claim that the Hayt-Wientge Mansion at 620 Paseo de la Cuma is the closest thing you will find that resembles the BATES MOTEL, in Alfred Hitchcock's *Psycho*. The Hayt-Wientge mansion, which stands atop the Rosario hill, is sometimes referred to as the "Psycho House."

Humorists say that all that mansion needs is a life-size cutout of Anthony Perkins standing at the entrance of the building. The mansion, if it resembles anything, approximates to a slight degree the haunted building in the Don Knot's film, *The Ghost and Mr. Chicken*. Aside from the long gables, the building does not look like the Bates Motel.

The Hayt-Wientge mansion was built in 1882 and is now a private residence. They don't make houses or mansions like that any more. It's on the National Register of Historic Places. The Hayt-Wientge mansion may look scary but it's free of things that "go bump in the night," when compared to La Posada and Julia Staab. However, Eve Wientge, a spiritualist of renown, lived in the mansion until her death in 1972. Anybody for a "Seance On a Wet Afternoon"? [13]

It's of interest that two Santa Fe stories, "Gravity Hill" and "The Donkey Lady," have similar plot lines to urban legends that are found in the San Antonio, Texas, area. You decide for yourself if these two tales are good or just plain bad high school scare stories.

Northeast of Santa Fe on a country lane that leads to the ski basin is an area of roadway called "Gravity Hill." A Santa Fe fable claims that Newton's Law of Gravity does not apply on this inclined motor way.

Down from the Ranger Station on Hyde Park Road is where Gravity Hill is located. It is alleged that a group of teenagers back in the

1950s or 1960s were pushing their stalled car up the Gravity Hill road. At the time of this incident the "Hill" was nameless.

The driver of a fast approaching car lost control of his vehicle and slammed into the teenagers and their stalled car. The teenagers died on the spot.

Today, if you put your car into neutral and are on the small inclined roadway that goes up Gravity Hill, your car will be nudged along by the teenage ghosts who lost their lives on this winding road.

Sadly, Hyde Park Road has had many tragic car accidents, but records indicate that this story has no merit. Yet, there are Santa Feans who will claim that before the Gravity Hill road was repaved, cars were pushed up the road's incline by an invisible force.

The "Donkey Lady" story first surfaced in Santa Fe and then in Albuquerque in the late 1950s. This Santa Fe urban legend concerns itself with a woman who was badly disfigured in a fire. The woman's fingers were burnt down into stub-like hooves. The trauma of the fire had damaged the woman's mental capacity, so she was cared for by her husband and loved ones.

When the Donkey Lady was left by a phone at her house, she would pick up the telephone when it rang. She would repeatedly "hee haw" into the phone's mouthpiece until one of her family members hung up the phone or the caller hung up out of fright.

The Donkey Lady "hee haws" were diabolical in sound and would frighten the listener. Teenagers who heard about the Donkey Lady would call her house in hopes she would pick up the phone and scare the teens with her unearthly braying.

The telephone number where the Donkey Lady lived would constantly be changed because her loved ones did not like the phone ringing around the clock. Also, the family members did not like the Donkey Lady being ridiculed.

By the early 1970s, the story and reports of the Donkey Lady had faded away. Perhaps the Donkey Lady was moved out of town, institutionalized, or died. Perhaps the story became too common and other falsehoods took its place. Coincidentally, in the early 1970s the tale of the Donkey Lady become part of the lore of San Antonio, Texas.

The San Antonio version has the Donkey Lady out and about at night, skulking through the lover's lanes of the area, as she tries to surprise and slay teenage couples as they smooch in their cars.

The San Antonio story is very far from the Santa Fe story. Datewise, it looks like Santa Fe can claim that it was the first town to have the tale of the Donkey Lady! Santa Fe's version of a deranged scarred woman who answers the phone, sounds just as implausible as that of a lover's lane type stalker. Hee haw!

THE MIRACLE AT SANTA FE

The Loretto Chapel at 207 Old Santa Fe Trail is a smaller version of the Saint Chapelle of Paris. In 1878, during the completion of the Chapel, a structural error was discovered. The Loretto Chapel did not have enough space for a planned staircase that was to link the choir loft with the ground floor.

The Catholic Sisters who governed the Loretto Chapel asked Santa Fe's carpenters and masons to figure out a solution as in how to build a staircase to the choir loft, which is twenty-two feet above the ground floor. After much planning, the Santa Fe builders concluded that it was impossible to fashion a stairway in any form due to the cramped proportions of the chapel.

There were only two options, either tear down part of the masonry and start all over again or use a ladder to gain access to the choir loft. Both ideas were dismissed. The Catholic Sisters then decided to pray a Novena in order to find a resolution to their problem. The Novena was made to St. Joseph, the patron saint of carpenters.

On the last day of the Novena, an elderly, bearded carpenter arrived with his donkey at the Loretto Chapel. The carpenter needed work and said that he could build a beautiful stairway to the choir loft with the dimensions that existed inside the chapel. The Catholic Sisters hired the carpenter and promised pay upon the completion of the job.

With his tools and saws the carpenter began his work. After six months the staircase to the choir loft was completed.

The carpenter had built a spiral staircase that was shaped like a DNA strand. The choir loft was now connected to the ground floor. The spiral staircase had thirty-three steps in it and two complete three hundred and sixty degree turns.

After completing his task, the carpenter did not claim his pay. He had mysteriously disappeared. The Catholic Sisters ran an ad in the Santa Fe newspaper in hopes of finding the carpenter, but there was no trace of the man.

Was this carpenter and the construction of the staircase something out of the realm of the Divine? The Sisters of Loretto finally concluded that the carpenter must have been St. Joseph.

Did the Novena bring a miracle to the Catholic Sisters? Perhaps, because there is no other stairwell like the Loretto staircase in the world. The Loretto staircase has no central support and no engineer can explain how it stands up or bears weight, yet it does. Also, the spiral staircase was put together with wooden peg-like nails. Furthermore, the wood that makes up the staircase is foreign to any classification. It's now known as Loretto Spruce wood, being that there is no other wood like it in this world.

It has been over a hundred years since the spiral staircase was completed and nobody has come forward and proved that a family member built or engineered the wooden monument. Is the staircase heavenly made or is the yarn more legend than truth? Take a look at the staircase and then decide. [14]

The Loretto Chapel Staircase

JOURNEY TO CHIMAYO

On Good Friday in 1810, the village of Chimayo, which is located thirty miles north of Santa Fe, experienced a miracle. A group of Penetentes, a Catholic lay group known for its devotion and fanaticism, saw a light glitter from an area near the outskirts of Chimayo.

The Penetentes ran to the exact spot where the light was seen, but the Penetentes were too slow and the light had vanished. One of the Penetentes got the idea to dig into the ground where the gleaming light had been. Other Penetentes joined in, and the group unearthed a large wooden crucifix.

It was a miracle, a cross in the ground, and a Holy light had shown them the way. The Penetentes took the crucifix to the church at Santa Cruz and left it on the altar.

The next morning the Penetentes were shocked to find that the crucifix had disappeared. The Penetentes went searching for the large cross and discovered it at the area where they first dug it up. The cross was taken back to the church and the same events happened the following day.

The Penetentes and the people of Chimayo concluded this was a heavenly sign and that a church should be built on the sight where the crucifix was found. Chimayo in 1810 did not have a church for Sunday mass. The villagers had to trek to Santa Cruz because that was where the closest church was located.

From 1810 to 1816, the Penetentes and the villagers of Chimayo labored and built a small church upon the ground where the large cross was found. The ground where the cross was found was left partly open. It is called *El Posito*.

The Catholics in the area concluded that the ground the Chimayo church was built on must have some type of sacred power. A few sickly people put some of the dirt from the El Posito onto their hurts and miraculously they were cured.

Soon Chimayo became the Lourdes of the Southwest. The dirt from the church at Chimayo produced miracle after miracle. The Chapel at Chimayo is filled with crutches and canes of those who were miraculously cured of their ills.

The church at Chimayo has become a world-renown pilgrimage sight for Catholics. On Holy Thursday through Easter Sunday the multitudes trek from Santa Fe to Chimayo. The pilgrimage is long and hard; the traveler walks highway shoulders, narrow paved roads, country fields, and dirt lanes.

The pilgrims march in all types of weather, be it scorching sunny days, rain-soaked nights, or blizzard conditions in order to pay homage at the church. There is no other pilgrimage like it in the United States.

Pilgrims go in groups or by themselves as they pray and exert themselves on a very physically demanding route. The roads into Chimayo are full of curves and steep tall hills. It is quite a sight to see the multitudes traipse toward Chimayo during Easter weekend.

The church at Chimayo is known as Santuario and has been named a National Historic Landmark. The Pilgrimage to Santuario de Chimayo is one of the most pleasant and simple spectacles of faith that anyone will ever witness. It is well worth a visit come Easter time. [15]

RECIPE FOR AN APPARITION

On the morning of October 5, 1977, Maria Rubio of Lake Arthur, New Mexico, was making burritos for her husband and children, when she noticed that a tortilla she had just made had the face of Jesus on it. The Rubio family was astounded. Maria cut the tortilla down so she could save the face of Jesus in a napkin.

Maria's skillet was made out of old scrap iron farm machinery. Before and after this event, there has never been a duplicate or near duplicate of Jesus on a tortilla by way of Maria's skillet.

No special chemicals or ingredients were added to Maria's tortilla recipe. It was just regular flour.

Maria and her husband Eduardo were born in Mexico and worked as farm laborers. Maria and Eduardo did not have a high level of education, but they had made the best of their opportunities in the United States.

To Maria, the tortilla with Jesus on it was a message from the Divine. The tortilla is the most common of Mexican food, feeding multitudes of the unwealthy.

The interpretation of Jesus on this tortilla was that Jesus loved the Rubio family very much. Likewise, Jesus loved the working poor who had little in food or creature comforts, but did their best to live a good life. The Bible states that Jesus loved the poor and his followers were people who made their living by the sweat of their brow.

The Jesus tortilla was exposed to the air for many days, yet it did not crumble or get moldy. The story of the tortilla spread and soon people from all over New Mexico and then from all over the country were coming to the Rubio's house to see the Jesus tortilla.

The Catholic Church deemed the Jesus tortilla a coincidence, not a miracle. One newspaper reporter in an insulting way referred to Maria's tortilla not as a picture of Jesus but rather an image of the boxer, Leon Spinx.

None of the criticism bothered the Rubio family. Maria put the Jesus tortilla in a glass picture frame where it sits today. The Rubios converted a shed at their house into a small shrine for the Jesus tortilla.

This haven is a well-kept carpeted room that is lit by electric candles; vases with fresh flowers decorate the chamber.

Lake Arthur, New Mexico, is not close to Santa Fe County. However, the tortilla story was included in this book because it sounds like a Santa Fe story. Anything and everything can happen in Santa Fe, which is known as "The City Different." [16]

2

MURDER: EXECUTIONS AND THE CULT

LEGITIMATE HATRED, THE 1890s FEUD

You may need a pencil and paper to keep track of who is who and which side did what, for this is a most complicated story! Santa Fe's great 1890s feud is Shakespearean in depth, but sadly there is very little myth or lore in it. The tale is tragically real.

On April 2, 1897, brothers Antonio and Francisco Borrego y Gonzales along with Laureano Alarid and Patricio Valencia were hung in the courtyard of the Santa Fe City Jail. The State Militia was called out and stood ready around the jail in case the people of Santa Fe stormed the gallows and freed the condemned men. The men on the gallows had received six stays of execution and the case went all the way to the Supreme Court.

The jail and gallows were located at what is now 121 Sandoval Street. A building and parking lot now occupy the area. This hanging was one of the most unpopular events in Santa Fe's history; it should never have happened.

In 1891, Francisco Borrego y Gonzales, after being slighted and insulted by the chiefs of the Democratic party, joined the Republican party. Consequently, many people followed Borrego y Gonzales' move and switched parties.

Borrego y Gonzales left the Democratic party with hard feelings because he had won the election of 1891 for City Coroner which carried with it the duties of Police Chief. When the City of Santa Fe was incorporated in late 1891, the election results were voided. The new rules of incorporation meant that the Coroner-Police Chief job became two jobs and more importantly these two jobs now became political appointee positions.

Democratic Mayor William Thorton decided that Borrego y Gonzales was not a "yes" man and picked two of his own men for the jobs of Coroner and Police Chief. Mayor Thorton appointed Jose Gallegos as County Coroner and Francisco Chavez as Police Chief (Sheriff) of Santa Fe.

In late 1891, at 200 West San Francisco, where a popular bar is now located, a promenade was held. By happenstance or on purpose, Gallegos ran into Borrego y Gonzales who was supervising the city dance. Harsh words were exchanged. Gallegos called Borrego y Gonzales a "vendigo."

Both men called each other out and a fist fight took place in the street. Borrego y Gonzales was getting the better of Gallegos when friends of Gallegos jumped into the fight and held Borrego y Gonzales' arms.

Borrego y Gonzales was defenseless and was getting beaten to death by Gallegos. With blood in his eyes, Borrego y Gonzales managed to break free for a moment and draw his pistol and shoot Gallegos in the head.

Gallegos fell to the street, dead, and his cronies scattered. Borrego y Gonzales was cleaned up and then taken to the city jail under a citizen's arrest.

At the jail, Borrego y Gonzales was chained to a pole. Jailer Juan Dominguez, who was a friend of the dead Gallegos, beat up the defenseless Borrego y Gonzales. Sheriff Chavez, the same man who had been appointed to the job by Mayor Thorton, reached the jail after hearing of the shooting and the arrest of Borrego y Gonzales.

Upon seeing Sheriff Chavez, Borrego y Gonzales complained about how he had been beaten by the jailer. Sheriff Chavez, who was also a friend of the dead Gallegos, went berserk and pistol-whipped the chained, defenseless man. Borrego y Gonzales survived the beatings and was charged with the murder of Gallegos.

Thomas Catron, a Republican lawyer who was an enemy of Mayor Thorton's Democratic machine, chose to defend Borrego y Gonzales. Catron's logic was, an enemy of my enemy is my friend.

Catron and Thorton were arch enemies. Both men competed against each other for political offices, civic power, and financial wealth. Previous to the beating and trial of Borrego y Gonzales, Catron had nearly been assassinated by an unknown trigger man. The gunman's bullets went through a window and narrowly missed Catron.

Catron checked around and his sources told him that Mayor Thorton had hired Sheriff Chavez to assassinate him. Whenever Catron could strike back at Mayor Thorton he would, thus Catron became the consul for Borrego y Gonzales and aptly defended him.

Borrego y Gonzales was tried in court for the murder of Gallegos and was found innocent by reason of self-defense. While in jail, Borrego y Gonzales was constantly bullied by Sheriff Chavez and his chums. At one time, Borrego y Gonzales was temporarily blinded due to a beating.

Upon completion of the trial, Borrego y Gonzales left Santa Fe for Colorado in order to recuperate from the injuries he received while in jail. There, Borrego y Gonzales recovered his eyesight and swore revenge on Sheriff Chavez.

Borrego y Gonzales was not some ruffian. He was a well-spoken man who had won elections and was involved in small mercantilist deals. Borrego y Gonzales had two teams of horses. He brought coal from Madrid in his wagons to Santa Fe, as well as wood from the mountains. Today, Borrego y Gonzales would be considered an independent heavy-duty trucker.

On May 29, 1892, ex-Sheriff Chavez was crossing the Santa Fe Denver railroad bridge by Guadalupe Church when he was gunned down. His dying words were, "Those brutes got me."

Wagging tongues put Borrego y Gonzales as the gunman who shot down Sheriff Chavez, being that Borrego y Gonzales had now returned from Colorado and was living at his house in Santa Fe. Borrego y Gonzales' brother Antonio, as well as Laureano Alarid and Patricio Valencia, were said to have acted as lookouts.

The autopsy on Sheriff Chavez revealed that a Winchester bullet of 300 grains had hit him along with a bullet of 249 grains that belonged to a Colt revolver. Apparently, Chavez was shot down by two assassins or his killer used two different weapons during the slaying.

Jailer Dominguez, upon hearing about Sheriff Chavez's death, concocted a plan to ambush Borrego y Gonzales. Dominguez, who had beaten up the chained Borrego y Gonzales, figured that he was next to get shot down.

Borrego y Gonzales lived in the house that is now a restaurant, located at 724 Canyon Road. In the 1890s, the area between St. Francis Cathedral and its present day parking lot was filled with trees and grass. Borrego y Gonzales walked daily through that grassy tree area as he commuted between his house and the Plaza.

Dominguez ambushed Borrego y Gonzales in that glade, but luck and skill were on Borrego y Gonzales' side.

Shots were exchanged and Dominguez fell dead. The authorities arrested Borrego y Gonzales for the murder of Dominguez. Consequently, Borrego y Gonzales was charged for the murder of Sheriff Chavez. Also indicted were his brother Antonio and his friends, Alarid and Valencia.

Catron again defended Borrego y Gonzales and the three other men. Catron was able to prove that the death of Dominguez was self-defense. However, the jury convicted the Borrego y Gonzales brothers along with Alarid and Valencia of the premeditated murder of Sheriff Chavez.

The jury that presided over the Chavez trial had been bribed by the new sheriff of Santa Fe, William Cuningham, who was an enemy of Catron's. In the legal world, Catron's defense of the four defendants was a work of art.

The trial lasted thirty-seven days. Nonetheless, the jury found the four defendants guilty and they were sentenced to death by hanging. If the jury had not been bribed, Catron would have won his case. The trial was held at the Coronado Building that is at 141 East Palace Avenue.

The verdict was appealed all the way to the Supreme Court, which refused to hear the case. The four men were hung on April 2, 1897. The authorities did not let the four men speak their last words on the gallows.

The Borrego y Gonzales brothers' graves are located in the Rosario Cemetery. Next to them are the unmarked graves of their two friends, Valencia and Alarid. Rosario Cemetery is located at the crossroads of Rosario and Paseo de Peralta. [17]

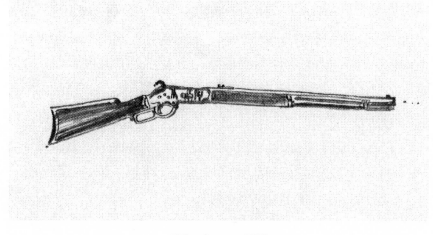

Winchester Rifle

THE OX BOW INCIDENT
OF SANTA FE

*T*he *Ox Bow Incident* is a 1943 Western movie, and the cast includes Henry Fonda, Dana Andrews, and Anthony Quinn. The film is about three cowboys who are charged with murder and rustling cows.

The mob that apprehends the three men does not thoroughly sift through the evidence and hangs the cowboys on flimsy proof. Only afterwards is it found that the three lynched men were innocent. *The Ox Bow Incident* is a very disturbing movie.

Sadly, Santa Fe had its own Ox Bow Incident in the early 1930s. Those who were alive during the legal lynching of Tom Johnson are ashamed and troubled at what transpired.

On the night of November 15, 1931, eighteen-year-old Angelina Jaramillo was raped, choked, and stabbed in the temple with a knife. Her death was long and brutal.

Angelina Jaramillo was a petite, beautiful, smart senior at Santa Fe's Loretto Academy. Her future seemed boundless for her bright personality radiated charisma. The teenager was recognized by many Santa Feans as a girl who had something special about her.

Angelina Jaramillo came from a very wealthy Santa Fe family, but a peculiar one as well. Her father, who died of tuberculosis in 1920, was Venceslao Jaramillo and was the first cousin of his wife (Angelina's mother), Cleofas Martinez.

A Catholic church dispensation was granted and the two first cousins Venceslao and Cleofas, were married in 1898. Were Cleofas and Venceslao truly in love with each other or was the marriage an old bourgeoisie ploy to keep the money and power inside the Jaramillo family?

Contrary to popular beliefs, marriage by first cousins was not common in the 1800s or early 1900. Lore has it that due to the Jaramillo and Martinez clan's wealth and power the Catholic Church sanctioned the marriage between the first cousins.

Cleofas Jaramillo, who was Angelina's mother, was a proud, domineering woman who was an accomplished Santa Fean. Cleofas founded the Sociedad Folklorica, which was a committee that made costumes for the Fiesta celebration as well as organized the Fiesta dances.

Cleofas was also an author who wrote books about northern New Mexico such as *Romance of a Little Village Girl* and *Shadows of the Past*. Widowed since 1920, Cleofas and her daughter Angelina lived at 142-144 Griffin Avenue. The Jaramillo house was a very long, elegant, big house.

Robert Alexander Smith was a Canadian from Montreal. He married Angelina Jaramillo's aunt, Mae Martinez, in 1919. Mae Martinez was Cleofas's younger sister by eighteen years. Robert Smith's penchant for booze and women led to Mae Martinez divorcing Robert Smith in 1929.

Angelina Jaramillo in the early 1930s had become friends with her ex-uncle, Robert Smith, who was seventeen years her senior. Robert Smith worked at various jobs in Santa Fe.

On the night of the murder, Angelina Jaramillo's mother claimed she was awakened by a light that flashed in her eyes. Cleofas rose from her bed to inspect her house and heard a noise from her daughter's bedroom.

Cleofas went into her daughter's bedroom and was struck in the head and then dragged into another room. Upon regaining her senses, Cleofas called for the police, but it was too late. Her daughter was dead.

After gathering evidence at the crime scene, Sheriff Jesus Baca drove his cruiser to Andrew's Garage to fill up his car's tank. Coincidentally, Sheriff Baca found gasoline attendant Oscar Churchill badly beaten. The gas station's cash register had been robbed and a car in the garage had been stolen.

This robbery was thought to be done by the man who had raped and murdered Angelina Jaramillo. The man who robbed the gas station was identified as Tom Johnson, a Negro, who was born in South Carolina. Tom Johnson had worked at Andrew's Garage as a gas pump service man.

Hours later in Albuquerque, Tom Johnson was captured. Tom Johnson was taken back to the Santa Fe jail where he confessed to robbing the gas station and stealing the car, but claimed he knew nothing about the Angelina Jaramillo murder.

During the interrogation at the jail, Tom Johnson was worked over by the constabulary. In spite of that, he kept to his story that he knew nothing of, nor had anything to do with, the murder of Angelina Jaramillo. The robbery was over owed or borrowed money that turned into a fight due to racial slurs.

Tom Johnson was labeled a liar and put on trial.

During the murder trial the prosecution maintained that glass shards from a green vase that was broken during the crime had Tom Johnson's finger prints on it. There was a major problem with this evidence. The prints and the "so-called" expert on the witness stand lacked credibility.

Tom Johnson was found guilty and sentenced to die in the Santa Fe prison, which was then located near the crossroads of St. Francis Drive and Cordova Road. Until the last minutes of his life, Tom Johnson proclaimed that he was innocent of Angelina Jaramillo's rape and murder.

On July 21, 1933, Tom Johnson became the first man in New Mexico to die in the electric chair. Previously, convicts were executed by hanging. To make sure all was in order before Tom Johnson was put into the death chair, a goat was strapped to the death seat and electrocuted.

Tom Johnson held a cross in his hand and he was led to the chair. The electrocution took eight agonizing minutes. The voltage had to be reduced during the execution for Tom Johnson's leg and head were smoking and burning. It would have been more merciful if he had been shot by a firing squad, rather than being on the edge of igniting into flames as he was electrocuted.

Watching Tom Johnson's execution, in the role of witness for the Angelina Jaramillo family, was Ben Martinez, the brother of Cleofas Jaramillo, Angelina's mother. Lore had it, that this uncle had been a power behind the trial. In retrospect, it seems that Ben Martinez was covering up for the crime that was committed by his ex-brother-in-law, Robert Smith.

After the execution, no one claimed Tom Johnson's body. The corpse was buried at the old penitentiary cemetery that is now near or under St. Francis Drive. Pen Road, which still exists, was the street that lead to the penitentiary and then out to the prison cemetery.

Was Tom Johnson telling the truth? Did a powerful wealthy family in Santa Fe have an innocent man executed? Who really killed Angelina Jaramillo?

After the execution of Tom Johnson, the Jaramillo family would not talk at all about the murder and the evidence.

One very disturbing story surfaced years after Tom Johnson's execution. During the 1940s, Santa Fe was swept by the talk of a supposed death bed confession by the man who murdered Angelina Jaramillo.

Angelina Jaramillo's ex-uncle, Robert Smith, supposedly confessed that he had raped and murdered the teenage girl. This uncle avowed that he let Tom Johnson take the blame.

If this is true, then Tom Johnson was lynched in the court system because he had no money, no influence, and was a Negro. Tom Johnson did have a criminal past but it's a long leap from robbery and assault to rape and murder, especially in the segregated United States of the 1930s.

A lot of things did not make sense with the murder trial. How did Tom Johnson know what room Angelina Jaramillo was in? The murderer had to have knowledge of the house floor plan. Would Tom Johnson know what room to go into? The Jaramillo house was a long, large, many roomed house.

During the murder trial, it was noted that all the doors and windows were locked at the Jaramillo house except one window. This window had a cactus and typewriter blocking the entrance into the house. Oddly, Tom Johnson's fingerprints were not found on the window or pane.

The prosecution claimed that the obstructed window area was where Tom Johnson entered the Jaramillo house, at night without the benefit of a light, and without knocking over the cactus or the typewriter. It is more likely that the murderer had a key to the house, and who would have a key to such a house? A family member.

Tom Johnson freely admitted to robbing the gas station and assaulting the station attendant, Oscar Churchill. In spite of that, Tom Johnson unfalteringly claimed he had not raped or killed Angelina Jaramillo.

Trial logic had it that Tom Johnson killed Angelina Jaramillo then went to a gas station and attacked the service station employee, Oscar Churchill. That trial logic of 1931 has no merit.

If Tom Johnson did the crime on Griffin Street, then why did he not steel valuables from that elegant house? After all, he stole money from the register at the gas station and he also stole a car from the gas station.

Another disturbing issue concerning the murder trial is that Cleofas Jaramillo waffled on identifying Tom Johnson as the murderer. Cleofas claimed that she only got a quick glance of the man who killed her daughter. Cleofas's description of what the murderer was wearing did not match what Tom Johnson was wearing when captured.

Being a Negro in 1930s America, having served in the Navy, Tom Johnson knew he would not get any tolerance from any jury when it concerned interracial rape and murder. Would a man of experience who grew up with Jim Crow laws risk his life over such an act?

Tom Johnson was not homicidal or stupid. He had traveled all over the United States, had an analytical mind, and was fond of building model airplanes in his spare time at his flat.

Today's crime experts state that most victims know the perpetrator of the crime. When it comes to incest, the majority of the time the crime is covered up as a family secret. With Cleofas being married to her first cousin, would she think that rape or sex amongst family members is right or wrong? Or something that must be concealed and not talked about?

Angelina Jaramillo probably recognized who it was that was attacking her and said she was going to tell, and then she was murdered for saying that. Did Cleofas lie when she claimed that she was either struck or fainted at the scene of the crime?

No matter how one looks at this murder, there are many holes in the prosecution's case. There is reasonable doubt galore.

Did Santa Fe stand by and let a man pay for a crime that he did not do? [18]

The Santa Fe Prison's Electric Chair

PLAZA BEHEADINGS

The Plaza was once the scene of a multi-beheading execution. On July 21, 1643, eight Spaniards convicted as accomplices in the murder of ex-Governor Luis De Rosas were marched out from the Palace of the Governors and beheaded on a platform that stood in the Plaza. The eight men, Antonio Baca, Francisco Salazar, Juan De Archuleta, Cristobal Enriquez, Diego Marquez, Nicolas Perez, Juan Ruiz de Hinojos, and Diego Martin Barba, were decapitated as a crowd witnessed the punishment conducted by Captain Alonso Pacheco y Heredia and his troops.

Research indicates that Santa Fe holds the record for the largest mass beheading of Europeans by Europeans in a Continental American town.

Santa Fe has seen it all, beheadings, lynchings, legal hangings, and death by electric chair. Lore has it that Francisco Salazar's severed head, while lying next to the gallows, mouthed or recited a Catholic prayer, the "Credo." Then life or reflexive muscular energy left Salazar's decapitated head. [19]

JOE QUESTION, THE FIVE THOUSAND DOLLAR MAN

Jesse Peter Merlan, whose radio name was Joe Question, was the gadfly of Santa Fe. The Joe Question Show, which Merlan produced, was a staple of Santa Fe radio from the early '70s through the late '80s. The Joe Question Show was a call-in radio program and was the best of its kind.

Listeners would be enthralled and outraged as know-it-all Joe Question aggressively spouted opinions on local and world events. The radio show was a vocal arena of ideas and facts. Joe Question was the show's champion verbal gladiator, who took no prisoners. The show had many incarnations on many different stations.

Northern New Mexicans and Santa Feans would call in to agree or challenge Joe Question on the topic that was being discussed. Many times, dial-in callers after being rebuked would become so angered that they would challenge Joe Question to a fist fight in some designated parking lot or back alley while on the air. Santa Fe lore has it that Joe Question would show up at the specified place but nobody else would.

The Joe Question show was so explosive that callers would sometimes lose control of their emotions and curse a blue streak over the live radio program. To counter that and keep the show on the air, the program at one station went to a ten second delay in order to bleep out foul words that an occasional disgruntled guest would yell out.

During the early '70s, the highlight of the show, aside from Joe Question's personality, was the five thousand dollar challenge. Joe Question would occasionally ask anybody to stump him with a question. If that person could baffle Joe Question, a five thousand dollar reward awaited the person who stymied him. Nobody ever got paid because Joe Question never got confounded by a question, be it political, history, sports, you name it.

Before Jesse Merlan became Joe Question, he had lived a very interesting life. Merlan was born in Brooklyn, New York, in 1913, the offspring of Sicilian immigrants. To counter Latin prejudice, Jesse changed his name from Mesina to Merlan.

As a young man, Merlan was a star athlete, having made the 1932 Olympic team as a shot putter, but he took no medal in the 1932 Los Angeles games.

Merlan made his fortune in the 1940s and 1950s by writing stories for various comic book companies. Prior to his Joe Question days, Merlan's claim to fame, besides being an Olympian, was that he invented many golden age comic book characters.

Throughout his writing career, Merlan freelanced for periodicals and newspapers. Merlan was an intellectual who could write comedy as well as serious articles for high-brow magazines.

Merlan had a photographic memory, and with all his imaginative cerebral firepower, the Joe Question character that Merlan invented became an easy fit. It's not clear if Merlan was like Joe Question all through his life or the role just took over Merlan.

His public persona became Joe Question, complete with black vest, string tie, and horn-rimmed glasses. Joe Question's aggressiveness over the radio waves often spilled over into his regular life.

In his Joe Question costume, Merlan would argue with Santa Feans he ran into, be it at a street corner or in a grocery store. During one city council meeting, Merlan became so enraged after losing an argument with zoning authorities that he threw a developer's blue prints onto the floor and stomped on them.

Another time Merlan was arrested for assault and waving a pistol in the air. This fracas happened when Merlan and his neighbors locked horns over a house's skylight that Merlan did not like.

Merlan, a.k.a. Joe Question, was mouthy, funny, and egotistical, but he was also kind and generous. Santa Fe lore alleges that Joe Question lent a lot of money to people who were in need. Furthermore, Santa Fe's La Residencia, a retirement home, was daily visited by Merlan who would drop off a load of day-old pastries from a local doughnut shop.

Mysteriously and tragically, on August 25, 1988, Jesse Merlan was murdered. He died after eating a bowl of cereal that was laced with Temik insecticide.

Merlan and his wife started their morning by having breakfast together. Both became ill after eating the contaminated cereal that tasted like straw. Merlan's wife survived the poisoning, but Joe Question died a slow painful death at St. Vincent Hospital.

The poison was identified as a federally restricted pesticide that is only available to licensed users. Merlan was not a licensed user of this insecticide, and he did not have anything similar to that kind of poison at his house.

What's more, Merlan and his wife had eaten from the cereal container the day before and had not gotten ill. Somebody had poisoned the cereal in the past twenty-four hours of August 24 to August 25, 1988.

As of today, the "Murder of Joe Question" is unsolved. Strangely, the Santa Fe Police Department did not classify the poisoning as a murder, but as a "suspicious death."

Whoever poisoned Joe Question had to know his home's layout, where the cereal was, and what Joe Question's eating habits were.

Santa Feans have many theories when it comes to Joe Question's homicide. Some say the murder had to be somebody in his family or from his inner circle of friends. Others say that it was a Mafia hit. Joe Question had a mysterious past and had supposedly lived a good part of the 1960s in Italy.

Most wagging tongues say that Joe Question's murderer was somebody he angered on his radio show, from years gone by.

Joe Question was Santa Fe's articulate gadfly. Like Socrates, he was done in by a form of hemlock. Joe Question was a brilliant man. His murder is one of Santa Fe's strangest. [20]

"Gadfly" Joe Question

A LITTLE WHITE MULE WITH MURDER

Throughout Prohibition, Santa Fe got its liquor from distilleries in Pojoaque and Nambe. Enterprising people risked the consequences of breaking the law and became bootleggers. The illegal home-brewed liquor was called "White Mule," because a swig of the potent liquid would make the drinker feel as if he had been kicked by a mule.

Santa Fe's Adolfo Esquibel, of 255 Read Street, sold White Mule to any thirsty Santa Fean who could afford it. On Sunday afternoon, March 13, 1933, Santa Fe Police Chief Apolonio Pino, got a report that Day Marshall Bob Burrus was drinking at the Esquibel house while on duty. Chief Pino and Deputy George Romero left the police station to go get Marshall Burrus.

Chief Pino and Deputy Romero arrived at the bootlegger's house on Read Street and found the residence to be filled with many people buying and drinking White Mule. Amongst the group of drinkers was

Marshall Burrus, who supposedly slurred his words as he tried to explain himself out of the jam.

Chief Pino embarrassed Marshall Burrus by demanding and reaching for the officer's badge in front of the crowd at the bootlegger's house. Pride took over and Marshall Burrus reacted badly. An argument ensued followed by curses and pushes.

During the heated altercation, Chief Pino quickly left the bootlegger's house and entered the outhouse. Was Chief Pino hiding from his deputy or had he been taken ill? Marshall Burrus followed and cursed at Chief Pino who stayed inside the outhouse.

Marshall Burrus then went back inside the bootlegger's house. Deputy Romero tried to calm down Marshall Burrus but for some unknown reason, be it insolence or being encouraged, Marshall Burrus again went outside and challenged Chief Pino at the outhouse door.

Suddenly gunshots were exchanged between the two. Witnesses could not tell who shot first, but the outhouse was riddled with incoming and outgoing bullets.

After both Chief Pino and Marshall Burrus had spent their pistol rounds, Marshall Burrus was escorted to his flat by some of the people who were at the bootlegger's house. Chief Pino then exited the outhouse with a bullet wound that proved to be fatal.

Hours later Marshall Burrus was arrested and was in time tried in court and found guilty of murder.

Shortly after this murder, Prohibition was repealed by an act of Congress and Santa Fe's days of bootleggers and White Mule were over. As for the story concerning Chief Pino's murder, there are too many gaps in it for it to be completely true.

Yes, there had been a gunfight in and around the outhouse. But what really happened at that bootlegger's house prior to Pino's murder? One wild story has it that Chief Pino was chased into the outhouse by Marshall Burrus and a gunfight then ensued.

Another murmur was that Chief Pino fired first and was gunned down while using the outhouse as cover. The true story about this murder never did come out because the many witnesses to the gunfight had too much to loose by telling the truth.

In any case, inebriation and bad leadership led to the death of Chief Pino. As far as history goes, Pino seems to be the only New Mexican of modern times who was killed while in an outhouse. [21]

The Outhouse on Read Street

THE SHAMAN'S SIDESHOWS IN TWO SANTA FES

On March 26, 1997, thirty-nine people of the Heaven's Gate cult were found dead in a mansion located in Rancho Santa Fe, California. The dead cult members, men and women, had committed suicide. The cult believed that upon their death they would be transmuted into new beings, like caterpillars that turn into butterflies.

In 1997, the Hale-Bopp comet lit up the night skies as it passed by earth. The cult's leader, Marshall Applewhite, interpreted the comet as a signal to transmute into another life form. Consequently, the cult along with Applewhite committed ritual suicide.

Lore and foggy data have it that the Heaven's Gate cult at one time was headquartered in Santa Fe, New Mexico. It is a fact that the cult actively recruited in Santa Fe.

Santa Fe is a Spanish word that means holy faith. Perhaps those words were instrumental in the cult setting up shop in Santa Fe and then killing themselves in Rancho Santa Fe. Whatever the connections or reasons why the cult picked areas with the name Santa Fe in it, will remain a secret because the answers died with the cult.

According to eerie Santa Fe lore, the night the last of the Heaven's Gate cult members killed themselves, another subgroup containing ex-members from the cult, locked themselves into a large rented Santa Fe hotel ballroom. This subgroup, proceeded with its rituals while chanting the names of some of the Heaven's Gate cult members. [22]

3

MAYHEM: MYSTERY, UFOs AND COWS

MEN FROM MARS?

UFO-ologists claim that New Mexico is the UFO capital of the world as far as sightings and phenomena are concerned. Why is New Mexico given this title? Because on July 4, 1947, a "Flying Disk" from parts unknown crash-landed outside Roswell, New Mexico. Some UFO-researchers dispute the date and go as far as to claim that the "flying saucer" was shot down, or there was a second crash that occurred in Corona, New Mexico.

UFO-ologists maintain that the military retrieved the bodies of the aliens who piloted the star ship. The technology from this crashed vessel was back-engineered, the upshot being this foreign science enabled the United States to pioneer the micro chip, fiber optics, Kevlar, night vision goggles, and other gadgets.

Regardless of that being true or false, one thing is certain: UFOs were sighted over Santa Fe way before the Roswell crash. It's also of note that northern New Mexico (Santa Fe County and surrounding areas) has been plagued by cow mutilations since the 1940s. UFO-ologists claim that these cow mutilations are a result of UFO activity.

SANTA FE WEST OF MARS, 1880

At dusk on Friday, March 26, 1880, local cowboys and a Santa Fe Railroad agent heard noises coming from the sky. The men looked up and saw a UFO. This sighting happened at Lamy, New Mexico, fifteen miles south of Santa Fe.

The UFO was described as a monstrous-sized craft that was fish shaped or like a cigar with a tail. A gondola-like bulge was seen at the bottom of the silvery vessel. The craft sailed across the sky toward the east at a high speed.

Before the craft moved out of sight, elegantly drawn letters that looked like ancient Egyptian symbols could be discerned on the outside of the vehicle. The craft was manned by humanoid-like occupants. These aliens were seen either looking down from the craft's walled walkways or peering from the vessel's bulkhead windows.

Legend has it that some of the creatures waved back at the shouting and motioning cowboys on the ground. Depending on the story, a cup, a saucer, or perhaps a flowerpot, fell from the craft and the object landed intact on the ground atop some large bushes. This object was brought to Santa Fe where it was sold to a mysterious stranger.

After the sighting, rumors circulated in Santa Fe about what the cowboys and railroad man had seen. Most Santa Feans thought that the flying machine had come from Cathay, which was another term for China.

This Santa Fe County UFO sighting pre-dates any other UFO sighting in the United States. Prior to this, there had been reports of flashing meteorite-like objects, but never a sighting that was this detailed.

It's of extraordinary interest that in 1896 to1897 there were more reports of this type of craft hovering over Sacramento, California, and Aurora, Texas. However, the Santa Fe sighting beats all these other UFO reports by at least sixteen years. Does that mean that aliens were interested in Santa Fe way back then? Yikes! [23]

UFO–1880

THE THINGAMABOB?

On March 24, 1933, Santa Feans and air mail pilots saw a strange object in the sky. Authorities said that it was a meteorite. The object stayed in the air for four minutes before disappearing. [24]

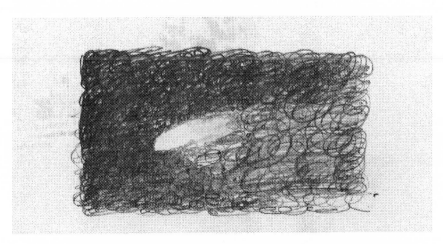

Meteor

THE THINGAMAJIG?

On March 7, 1951, a UFO was seen over Santa Fe headed in a northeast direction. The craft was described as extremely bright. The UFO was seen from La Junta, Colorado, to Roswell, New Mexico. A window-rattling noise marked the disappearance of the UFO as it vanished near Roy, New Mexico. Again, the experts said it was a meteorite. [25]

DOS HOMBRES Y UN UFO

On November 6, 1957, Joe Martinez and Albert Gallegos were driving down Santa Fe's county roads toward Cerro Gordo, when they spotted a UFO. The craft flew at a low altitude toward the vehicle of Martinez and Gallegos. Suddenly the interior of their car was illuminated, a strange noise was heard, and the vehicle's engine went dead. Likewise, but it was not discovered till later, Martinez's and Gallegos' wrist watches froze up, as well as the car's clock.

After what seemed like less than a minute, the bright UFO flew off in a southerly direction. Were Martinez and Gallegos correct in describing what happened? How strange that all the time pieces stopped functioning.

Perhaps both men were wrong in their estimates of how much time had elapsed, or were they both abducted and have no memory of it?

Or was this story a big lie? Maybe, maybe not. Many people in Santa Fe and New Mexico reported seeing a UFO during the period of

November 5 through November 8, 1957. With all the corroborating sightings of a UFO craft, it's very likely that Martinez and Gallegos are telling the truth. [26]

THE SAGA OF APRIL 27, 1964

The following story is a mixture of lore and facts. Nonetheless, there is so much evidence concerning this "Close Encounter" that perhaps a UFO really did land at La Madera, which is north of Santa Fe, on the night of April 27, 1964.

Twenty-year-old Don Adams of Edgewood, which is on the western border of Santa Fe County, was driving his car down a dirt road on April 27, 1964, when he saw a UFO slowly move across the night sky. Curiosity got the better of Adams, and he turned his car around and raced down the dirt roads in hopes of getting a better look at the vessel.

Eventually, Adams was able to catch up to the UFO and drive his car under the hovering craft. The UFO was about twenty-five feet long and appeared to emit a glowing fluorescent green color. With a flash of light the interior of Richardson's car was illuminated, and the engine of his car stalled.

As Adams observed the craft, he grabbed his six-shooter and got out of his vehicle.

Adams fired his pistol at the craft and shot off all his revolver's chambers. Adams quickly reloaded and again fired at the UFO until he again had emptied his pistol of bullets. Another version of this story has Adams armed with a rifle that held twelve cartridges.

The UFO then flew off. Did Adams' shots damage the craft? Why did this UFO not return fire on Adams? Or were the bullets that Adams fired at the UFO the equal of a Daisy BB gun being fired at an elephant? Then again, perhaps Adams' bullets knocked out some type of system in the UFO, thus saving Adams' life.

Is it possible that Adams was abducted and he has no recollection of it? Is the Adams account an embellished story or is it hogwash? One thing is certain, stranger things happened that night.

North of Santa Fe, in the La Madera area, people reported an egg-shaped UFO in the night skies. Coinciding with this UFO sighting were reports of livestock stampeding down the dirt roads in a panicked headlong flight. What spooked them?

Either the animals had become terrified and broke out of their corrals, or some pranksters had purposely let the animals out of their enclosures. The next day, in a La Madera field, the authorities and civilians found large circular burnt areas along with depressions that resembled the pod shoes or landing gear of some type of craft.

Some people claimed they saw mountain lion-like paw prints around the burnt areas in the large field. Coincidences, tall tales, as in *Lion Men from Mars*, or were the eyewitness accounts of the strange happenings the truth?

Coinciding with this encounter was police officer Lonnie Zamora's April 24, 1964, encounter with a UFO outside of Socorro, New

Mexico. Zamora's encounter made national headlines. Pod marks and burnt ground were found where Zamora testified that he had seen a UFO take off. Zamora's description of the UFO sounded very similar to what was supposedly seen over Santa Fe on April 27, 1964.

Putting all the lore and facts together, maybe there was something over Santa Fe on that spring night in 1964. Maybe that something landed in La Madera, and maybe that something had some of Don Adams' bullets in it. Wink, wink.

Was that 1964 craft the same UFO that Gallegos and Martinez reported in 1957? Or was the 1964 story just half truths and pranks? [27]

Santa Fe County UFO

THE DAWN PATROL

On March 23, 1970, at 5 A.M., a UFO was sighted over Santa Fe by numerous people. Prior to this, the UFO had been sighted over Las Vegas, New Mexico. The UFO was described as a flashlight-like craft that kept casting a light toward the west. The UFO was observed for forty-five minutes before it faded in the morning light.

Why are there so many reports of UFOs in March and April over the Santa Fe area? From the 1880s to the 1970s these two months have been loaded with UFO sightings.

Are these sightings the prelude to something ominous or is it just spring fever and mass hysteria? [28]

THE COSMIC WATERGATE!

UFO-ologists maintain that certain government agencies and national leaders cover up dangerous alien activity on the scale of a "Cosmic Watergate." These UFO believers or hobbyists contend that spin doctors and debunkers manufacture excuses or make fools out of people who report abductions, cow mutilations or UFO sightings.

UFO-ologists claim that the cow mutilations that hit Santa Fe County and other nearby counties in the 1990s were directly related to UFO activity. A cow mutilation is a cow that has been killed, drained of its blood, and had specific organs removed with "laser-like surgical precision."

The buzzwords of this phenomena are "surgical precision." The killing and mutilation of a cow or cows generally occurs at night. There have been no witnesses as to what or who is behind the mutilation.

Footprints or tire tracks are not found around the mutilated cow and no sign of struggle is evident. According to UFO-ologists, whatever killed the cow acted with lethal quickness.

Some ranchers who have handled their mutilated cows have reported that they have become ill afterwards. Was the illness psychosomatic, or was the sickness brought on by the smell of the rotting carcass?

The standard cow mutilation has the cow missing its rectum. Under the mutilated cow's tail, the anus has been enlarged to a frisbee-like proportion. The cow's anus tissue area looks like something used an oblong circular can to cut the cow's inners out. The bored out wound does not leak blood and there is no jagged cut marks or tears. The mutilated cow, female or male, has its sex organs removed. These organs are cleanly and bloodlessly amputated.

The mutilated cow usually has one eye missing, sometimes two. No blood is found dripping from the eye socket and no blood is found in the eye socket.

Some mutilations include the removal of the tongue, once again no blood coming from its mouth. Sometimes there is a small hole in the chest area, and from this wound the cow's heart has been removed.

Cow mutilations differ when it comes to the hide. Occasionally the hide of the cow's face has been peeled back and other times there is no evidence that the cow's hide has been mangled. Other than this difference, there is very little deviation in how a cow is mutilated.

Since the 1970s, cow mutilations have been reported in the United States media. Broadcasters and authors claim that the first animal mutilation occurred in 1967, others say much earlier.

The oddity of this report is that it was not a cow that was reported mutilated by the media in 1967, it was a horse named Lady.

On September 9, 1967, Burl and Nelie Lewis of the San Luis Valley, Colorado, reported that they found Lady, their Appaloosa mare, mutilated at their ranch. Lady's hide was missing from its neck up. The mare's organs had been removed and its blood drained.

Pod marks and scorched earth were found near the horse's carcass. A strange light was reported in the night sky before Lady was found mutilated.

Santa Fe County has made a jumble of the time line that investigators use in covering cow mutilations. Santa Fe can lay claim to having the first cow mutilation in the United States, perhaps the world.

Santa Fe lore asserts that in 1947, twelve miles west of Santa Fe, in La Cienega, Willie CdeBaca found one of his cows mutilated. His grandson, Felipe CdeBaca, had previously told his family that he had seen glowing globes on the mesa west of town.

Cow mutilations in and around Santa Fe became a serious problem in the late 1940s. On August 13, 1950, the District Attorney hired investigator Manuel Montoya to examine and appraise the cow mutilations that were occurring in northern New Mexico. At that time, the cow mutilation phenomena in the Santa Fe area was called, "the stabbing and slashing of cattle."

In the 1970s alone, there were over ten thousand cows reported mutilated in the United States. By 1975, every state west of the Mississippi had reports of cow mutilations. This phenomena was also reported in Canada, Mexico, Argentina, and Brazil.

Not one person has been caught in connection with the killing and mutilating of cattle. Another odd thing about cow mutilations is they seem to come in clusters.

In the late 1970s a rash of cow mutilations were reported in the hamlets north of Santa Fe.

Rancher Elie Hronich lost thirteen cows to mutilation deaths over a sixteen month time span. Hronich has ranched for over thirty years and has seen a lot of dead cattle in his time, but when it comes to mutilated cows, Hronich does not have an answer for it.

On August 19, 1994, Max Cordoba of Truchas discovered three of his cows dead and mutilated in his pasture. All three cows were thought to be pregnant. Eerily, the carcasses showed no sign of struggle and there was no sign or evidence of human activity around the three dead cows.

On September 19, 1994, Eddie and David Cook of Pecos found their colt one hundred feet from their house. It had been killed and mutilated.

One cow mutilation investigator, who was a retired Sandia Laboratory scientist, worked with the University of Iowa's veterinary lab in trying to determine what types of tools or procedure were used in mutilating a cow. To do this, the investigator and his team cut into a carcass at the veterinary lab.

The result of this experiment was that after eight hours of working on a cow's carcass, the veterinary team could not duplicate the wounds found on mutilated cows.

The conclusion was that whatever was doing the mutilating had much better instruments than the ones found in a state-of-the-art veterinary lab. More than that, if a cow could not be mutilated in the lab after eight hours of work, then how could a cow in the field be mutilated in one night? [29]

Cow Mutilation

DEATH RAY FROM THE MOON?

On August 20, 1994, Larry Gardea, who worked for rancher Estevan Sanchez, had an encounter with a cow mutilation! Rate this experience in the "believe it or not" category. Gardea was in Lujan Canyon at about 5:30 P.M. looking for the herd of cows that he was in charge of. Gardea found the herd and noticed the carcass of a cow that had been recently mutilated.

Gardea then heard a strange noise that came from behind a stand of trees. The noise was a grinding sound that resembled the din an arc welder makes when amalgamating metal. He then witnessed a cow being dragged back into the stand of trees by a beam of light.

Gardea, who was armed, shot off two rounds from his 30.06 rifle into the area of the woods where the beam was coming from. The arc welder noise stopped, the beam of light vanished, and the cow was released.

Gardea became frightened and drove back to his house and called the police.

Deputy Greg Laumbach and Gardea returned to Lujan Canyon and discovered that one cow had been mutilated. The carcass had its rectum bored out, its sexual organs and tongue had been removed, and, as always, there were no tracks around the mutilated cow.

The duo also discovered that a cow was missing from the herd. It was not known if the cow that Gardea had rescued from that beam of light was the cow that was missing. As for what was behind the stand of trees, Deputy Laumbach and Gardea found nothing.

Is it conceivable that all these UFO stories are just tall tales? Are some of these stories legit? One thing is certain, a lot of cows have turned up dead in these parts and many people have seen some inexplicable things in the skies over Santa Fe. [30]

4

THE ATOMIC BOMB AND CRIME

THE GUY NEXT DOOR IS A SPY!

The following information is murky, frightening, and fascinating. Certain aspects may be pure hokum and then again it may be the truth.

In 1943, the United States' premier military laboratories were built in Los Alamos, which was then part of Santa Fe County. The scientists and military personnel at these laboratories were given the job of creating the Atomic Bomb. The code phrase "Manhattan Project," was used to encompass all of what went on in developing the Atomic Bomb throughout World War II.

Santa Fe lore has it, that during the Manhattan Project days of World War II, the Coronado Pharmacy was a Soviet spy safe house. The Coronado Pharmacy was located in the Coronado building at 141 East Palace Avenue. Before New Mexico gained statehood into the Union, the Coronado building was known as the Territorial Court House.

Was the Coronado Pharmacy a key cog in the Soviet spy network as in a rendezvous point? One curious fact that cannot be dismissed, is that the Santa Fe headquarters for the Manhattan Project was located in the Trujillo Plaza at 109 East Palace Avenue. The Trujillo Plaza building is just a few hundred yards down the street from the Coronado building.

Legendary Soviet spy Master Pavel Sudoplatov, who had been working in Soviet intelligence since 1919, released a memoir with the help of his son Anatoli Sudoplatov and ghost writers Jerrold and Leona Schecter in the mid-1990s. The book was titled, *The Memoirs of an Unwanted Witness–a Soviet Spymaster*. This book, along with reporter Kay Bird's 1994 article in the *Santa Fe Reporter*, brought the following information to light.

Sudoplatov claims that the top Soviet spy in Santa Fe was a Joseph Grgulevich. According to Sudoplatov, Grgulevich was a hero of the USSR. Before coming to Santa Fe, Grgulevich had fought in the Spanish Civil War, and had liquidated many people in Lithuania. This Santa Fe spy spoke fluent English and Spanish. Grgulevich opened a Santa Fe pharmacy in 1940 as his front, so it has been said.

Bird's research found that in 1940, Santa Fe had five pharmacies, two opened in 1940. The first was opened by a George Reed. He is listed in the 1938 Santa Fe directory. Reed had a wife and his records seem to be in order. Anatoli Sudoplatov told Bird, "That he doubted that Grgulevich would have brought his wife on a mission."

Bird then found that Arthur Reust opened the Coronado Pharmacy in 1940. Furthermore, Reust's employment record shows a gap that cannot be accounted for from 1930 to 1940.

Reust died in 1968. Perhaps the Coronado Pharmacy was used without Reust's knowledge as a place that masked Soviet espionage.

At any rate, Santa Fe was rumored to be a hive for Soviet spy activity. It is a fact that during World War II the Manhattan Project secrets were stolen and passed on in Santa Fe. [31]

THE BRIDGE OF SPIES

The Delgado Street Bridge is a very narrow two-way span that has no sidewalks. It crosses the Santa Fe River near Canyon Road and is one of the oldest overpasses in Santa Fe.

In 1945, the Manhattan Project's atomic bomb secrets were said to have been stolen from a military lab in Los Alamos. According to Santa Fe lore, this data was handed off from spy to spy under the Delgado Street Bridge. The spy who received the data succeeded in getting that top secret information to the USSR.

Why did the two spies meet under the Delgado Street Bridge? Legend has it that the area under the span was the best secret place for a face to face meeting in Santa Fe.

Hobos or teenage lovers did not meet or hang out under the bridge because the area under the overpass was infested with water snakes. Due to the bridge's two-way traffic flow and its tight constraints, pedestrians do not skylark or sightsee from this old causeway.

The Delgado Street bridge is still in use. There is no marker at the bridge telling what transpired under it in 1945. [32]

THE BIG STEAL

La Conquistadora is a three foot tall wooden statue of the Virgin Mary. The statute wears a gold crown and holds a crystal rosary. La Conquistadora is referred to as SHE, by many of the old Catholic Santa Feans who trace their roots back to the days of the Spanish Conquistadors.

La Conquistadora was carved in Spain and brought to Mexico by galleon and then to Santa Fe by caravan in 1625. Santa Feans of that time used the statute as a symbol in their Catholic worship and the icon was utilized as a baptismal conversion tool when preaching to the Indians of the area.

The name La Conquistadora was given to the statute in 1625, as "Our Lady of the Conquest." Those who named her were the Conquistadors, a Spanish term for soldier-conquerors. The Conquistadors believed that La Conquistadora watched over them.

In 1680, the Indians of New Mexico revolted and killed many Spanish settlers. The surviving Spaniards rallied at the Palace of the Governors, which was not only the capital building but also a fortress.

After many bloody battles and a siege, the Spaniards retreated from Santa Fe. The Spaniards escaped to what is now El Paso, Texas.

In the retreat, the Santa Feans took all the food and water they could carry, along with armaments, and also La Conquistadora. Santa Fe was then occupied by the Indians for twelve years. During this time most of the Spanish buildings were burnt down and anything Catholic was defiled.

In September of 1692, Captain Diego De Vargas lead a column of Conquistadors back to Santa Fe. Their mission was to reconquer what was lost twelve years previously. The Conquistadors brought the statute of La Conquistadora with them.

The Conquistadors bivouacked on what is now Rosario Cemetery, located at the crossroads of Guadalupe and Paseo de Peralta. De Vargas prayed that the Indian armies that occupied Santa Fe would surrender rather than fight. De Vargas made a promise to Jesus, if the Indians surrendered in a bloodless manner, De Vargas would honor La Conquistadora with a procession and build a chapel to the Madonna.

Soon after that, the Indians surrendered to the Conquistadors and the reconquest was peaceful, and this was thought to be a miracle. As the Conquistadors were breaking camp to march into Santa Fe as the victors, La Conquistadora seemed welded by some Divine force to the ground. This event was interpreted by De Vargas that that was where the Chapel to La Conquistadora was to be built.

Years later after lasting peace had come to the area, mini revolts flared up after the reconquest. A shrine area was built to La Conquistadora inside the church that preceded Saint Francis Cathedral. Eventually, the Rosario Chapel was built. This is where it was said that La Conquistadora was welded to the ground by some heavenly force.

To honor La Conquistadora, every year a walking cavalcade leaves Saint Francis Cathedral with the Madonna and proceeds to the Rosario Chapel. La Conquistadora stays for a number of days at the Rosario Chapel while a Novena is prayed.

When the Novena is completed, La Conquistadora is returned in a procession to the Cathedral.

On the night of March 18, 1973, La Conquistadora was stolen from the Chapel at Saint Francis Cathedral. Santa Fe police detectives surmised that the thieves had hidden inside the cathedral and after everyone had left, climbed onto the altar and stole Santa Fe's Madonna.

On April 7, 1973, church officials at the cathedral received a ransom note in poorly written Italian. "$150,000 for La Conquistadora," read the note. "If terms are accepted signal us at 4:45 P.M. by ringing the bells of the cathedral ten times." The Santa Fe community was galvanized to get back La Conquistadora.

A major reward was then offered to anybody who helped in the retrieval of the Madonna. The reward offer worked. An anonymous person told the authorities who had stolen La Conquistadora and the police soon arrested two local male teenagers and found the Madonna in a cave south of Los Lunas.

The two teenagers who stole the statute pleaded guilty and were given the maximum sentence for larceny. Their sentences sent out a message to all potential thieves. To paraphrase singer/songwriter Jim Croce, "You don't step on superman's cape, you don't spit into the wind, and you don't mess around with" Santa Fe's most treasured Catholic icon![33]

5

SANTA FE: COLONIAL TIMES AND THE WILD WEST

THE FOUNDING OF SANTA FE

Santa Fe was founded in 1610 by Spanish settlers under the command of Captain General Pedro de Peralta. Santa Fe was to be the capital of the Spanish Kingdom called New Mexico. The colonists of Santa Fe were given the job of harvesting the natural resources of the area and converting the Indians to Catholicism.

The site for Santa Fe was not chosen haphazardly, like somebody throwing a dart onto a large map and saying here is where we build. The site was chosen because the Indian Pueblos were located nearby, and the area was bountiful in water and resources.

This location insured its colonists that they would be able to dominate its Indian trade partners and, if need be, its Indian enemies.

The original town plan of Santa Fe was based on the city planning ordinance of King Philip II's 1573 Law of the Indies. The mandate stated that a city or town must have a starting place, and that starting place must be the town square.

Today, as in 1610, the Plaza is the start and center of Santa Fe. [34]

SERFS AND TAXES

Encomienda was the term for a land grant that was given to a Spaniard by the Spanish King and in some cases by the Spanish Governor of New Mexico. The land grantee was given "a certain" amount of land and all the Indians found on this land became the grantee's peons. An annual "tribute" was levied onto the man who was given the land grant.

That tribute would be paid to the Governor, who in turn would divide the amount into tribute payments. These tribute payments would then be sent to the King in Spain, to the local public works and to the Catholic Church, etc. It was a primitive tax system but it worked.

The encomienda also stressed that it was the responsibility of the grantee to bring Catholicism by way of conversion to all the Indians found on his land grant. The grantee was supposed to help the Catholic Church in any way possible in the area of religion. It's of note that a major part of Santa Fe lies on an old Spanish land grant.

CONFESS

In 1628, Luis de Rivera traveled with a wagon train along the Camino Real, which means the "Royal Road." The Camino Real begins in Vera Cruz, Mexico, and ends in Santa Fe. During this trek, Rivera confessed to a Catholic Padre who was in the caravan, that he had made a deal with the Devil while living in Mexico.

Rivera said he had signed his name in a book with his own blood. This book belonged to a man who knew about demonology and practiced the dark arts. Rivera's signature meant that the Devil would claim his soul when he died. In return for his soul, the Devil would grant Rivera's wishes.

All Rivera wanted was to be a great cowboy and acquire some creature comforts. Rivera soon changed his mind and now wanted out of his deal with the Devil. He feared that when he died his soul would be damned into Hell.

When the caravan reached Santa Fe, the Padre reported Rivera to the Catholic authorities and Rivera was arrested and sent back to

Mexico City in chains. In Mexico City, Rivera stood before the Inquisition tribunal.

Rivera confessed his guilt and begged for leniency. The Inquisition had mercy on Rivera; his punishment was penance and public service. Apparently Rivera's confession and appeals for pardon found a soft spot in the Inquisitors' hearts.

Rivera was incredibly fortunate. Very few men ever convinced the Inquisition tribunal that they were no longer a threat or evil. The majority of people who were brought before the Inquisition were later broken by physical torture and died under duress or while in prison.

Either Rivera was telling the truth and he was truly sorry for his "deal" with the Devil, and the Inquisitors could see this, or Rivera was a great con man and he had the "luck of the Devil" with him. [35]

Burros

THE INQUISITION

Governor Don Bernardo Lopez de Mendizabal was an open-minded, pragmatic, irreligious, colonial ruler. Consequently, he made many enemies during his reign as governor. From the Palace of the Governors, Mendizabal commanded New Mexico from 1659-1661. Mendizabal wanted to keep peace between the Spaniards and the Indians in order to make Santa Fe and the outlying province a profit-bearing land.

Mendizabal gave permission to the nearby Pueblo Indians that they could perform a sacred Kachina dance on the Plaza. Several Santa Feans saw the Kachina dance as a work of the Devil. For allowing the Kachina dance, Mendizabal was considered by some Santa Feans to be a heretic.

The Spanish Inquisition was a Catholic Church court that was set into place to protect the Catholic faith. The Inquisitor court was founded in Spain in 1478. As the Spanish Empire expanded, so did the

Inquisition. The Inquisition came to the New World and governed Santa Fe from its Holy Office in Mexico City.

Those in Santa Fe who were loyal to the ideas of the Inquisition did not approve of Mendizabal's actions. These would-be Santa Fe Inquisitors were not powerful enough to arrest the governor of New Mexico by themselves, so they wrote to the Holy Office in Mexico City.

When the Holy Office received reports of Mendizabal letting Pueblo Indians dance a Kachina ceremony on the Plaza, orders were cut to bring Mendizabal and his wife Teresa to Mexico City in chains.

On August 26, 1662, Mendizabal and his Italian wife Teresa were arrested and sent to Mexico City in shackles. Mendizabal lost his rank and all his property in Santa Fe was seized.

Teresa defended her husband and, in time, the charges against her were dropped, but not before Mendizabal died in the Mexico City Inquisitor prison.

With revenge on her mind, Teresa wrote an essay to the Inquisitor council revealing the vice that her husband's accusers were themselves involved in. Teresa's long letter was done out of vengeance, in hopes that the Santa Feans who were responsible for her husband's imprisonment and death would lose their property and be taken to Mexico in chains and tortured.

The next governors of New Mexico instituted policies toward the Pueblo Indians that went from bad to worse. Major transgressions by militant Pueblo Indians or by nomadic tribes who raided the Pueblos were overlooked. European greediness and uneven justice from the capital in Santa Fe plus droughts caused some of the Pueblo Indians to become pawns to rabble-rousing Indian holy men. The upshot of this was the Indian uprising of 1680.

The Indian revolt of 1680 drove the Spaniards out of New Mexico. Not until 1692 were New Mexico and Santa Fe reconquered by the Spaniards.

New Mexico's history in the late 1600s proves that if there had been more Mendizabal-like leaders in positions of power, events would have been much different. A lot of blood would not have been shed and a lot of suffering would have been avoided. [36]

Conquistador

APPLY THE CORDS

During Spanish Colonial rule, the Plaza had public floggings, laughing stocks, and criminal executions. The Plaza was also home to a small daily marketplace and public announcements were made by the town crier.

In 1643, eight Spaniards were condemned to death; their crime was murder. These men were executed in the Plaza by way of decapitation. The condemned were given the choice of death by garrote or blade. The garrote is a piano wire with wooden handles at each end. Death by garrote has the condemned man tied to a chair as he is strangled. Spanish justice was cruel but effective. [37]

IT PAYS TO HAVE
THE RIGHT SKILLS

One-legged Diego DeVelasco (lore has it that he was peg-legged) murdered Miguel Herrera on the Plaza in 1712. The initial argument between the two men started after Herrera made comments to DeVelasco about his livestock wandering over land boundaries.

Curses and threats were exchanged between the two men, and combat ensued after Herrera made remarks about DeVelasco's wife's sexual conduct. During the brawl DeVelasco killed Herrera. One wonders if DeVelasco used his wooden leg to brain Herrera.

A crowd quickly gathered to arrest DeVelasco as he stood over the body of Herrera. DeVelasco, thinking that he would be lynched, ran to a Catholic church that was located at the site of the present-day Saint Francis Cathedral.

Once inside the church DeVelasco claimed sanctuary. Throughout Spanish Colonial days, Santa Feans and the constabulary believed that a church was a holy place and it could not be defiled by an arrest.

DeVelasco stayed inside the church for a year. Finally the governor of New Mexico passed sentence on DeVelasco without a trial. DeVelasco was sentenced to do community service and to live at the Palace of the Governors' guard house for a short time.

DeVelasco was guaranteed that he would not be hung, strangled, whipped, or put into the stocks for the murder of Herrera. The reason DeVelasco got such a lenient sentence was because he was the only master carpenter in Santa Fe.

Santa Fe and the surrounding areas needed DeVelasco's services badly. DeVelasco cheated punishment and lived out his life without further mishaps. Back then, as today, it pays to have the right job. [38]

LADY GODIVA IN THE PLAZA

In 1716, Anna Maria Romero called another Santa Fe woman a whore in the presence of that woman's husband. Romero was tried and sentenced to two years in exile in Albuquerque. It was decreed that before Romero was banished, she must ride a horse around the Plaza and the public streets of Santa Fe. While doing this, Romero was ordered to have a gag in her mouth and be naked from the waist up. [39]

THE DEVIL MADE ME DO IT

In 1720, Ysidro Sanchez pleaded guilty to stealing merchandise from a royal storehouse on the Plaza. Sanchez pleaded for mercy. His excuse was, "The Devil made me do it." [40]

THE SANTA FE TRAIL

Prior to 1821, Santa Fe was considered a hermit kingdom. Spanish law prohibited trade with foreign merchants, be it English, French, or Americans. In September of 1821, after a bloody war, Mexico gained independence from Spain and Santa Fe became part of Mexico.

Santa Fe's Governor Facundo Melgares no longer had to follow Spanish dictates, and he opened up trade between Santa Fe and the United States, and the Santa Fe Trail was born. The Trail at first was just a series of water holes and the easiest route one could use in traveling from Franklin, Missouri, to Santa Fe.

As commerce between Franklin, Missouri, and Santa Fe grew, the Trail went from a path to a grooved dirt road that cut through the Southwest wilderness. For fifty-nine years the Trail was used as a mercantile passageway.

In 1821, Franklin, Missouri, due to its location, became the premier inland American trade city. Likewise, Santa Fe, due to its location, became the key trade city in the Southwest. The growth and wealth that would pour into these two cities over the next fifty-nine years could not have happened if it was not for the Santa Fe Trail.

The first trader to come down the Trail in a wagon convoy was William Becknell. His caravan consisted of twenty-three wagons and a cannon. Becknell's total cost for his wagon convoy was $35,000.

That amount included everything: goods, livestock, wagons, pay for the drivers, etc. After selling his goods in Santa Fe, Becknell returned to Franklin, Missouri, with $180,000 in profit.

Products brought into Santa Fe were resold again throughout the Southwest and Mexico. Santa Fe was not only the end of the Santa Fe Trail, but it was also the start of the Camino Real, which means "The Royal Road."

As mentioned earlier, the Camino Real ran from Santa Fe to the port city of Vera Cruz. Along the Camino Real were the cities of Chihuahua and Mexico City.

The Santa Fe Trail was a turnpike for small and large caravan trains. In 1860 alone, a minimum of three thousand wagons rolled into Santa Fe, along with over twenty-eight thousand oxen and six thousand mules.

Great risks were taken and great profits were made by people who traveled the Santa Fe Trail. A wagon that cost $150 in Missouri would be unloaded in Santa Fe and resold for $750.

It was common for donkey trains of four hundred or more animals to be herded from Santa Fe to Missouri and sold for profit. The famous Missouri Mule was the result of livestock bought in Santa Fe and convoyed to Missouri.

The only trade that was outlawed on the Santa Fe Trail was that done by the Comancheros. These people were renegades who traded with the Comanches. The Comancheros bought their guns, ammunition, and liquor in Santa Fe and then traded these goods to the Comanches for cattle and horses. The horses and cattle that the Comanches bartered with were animals that they had stolen or killed for in their raids into Texas.

The Mexican War of 1846 was ended by the Guadalupe y Hidalgo Treaty of 1848. The upshot of this was that Mexico surrendered Santa Fe and the Southwest to the United States. This meant that Mexican trade tariffs no longer applied to items brought into Santa Fe. Therefore, more profits were reaped by the merchantmen who came down the Trail.

The Santa Fe Trail was anywhere from seven hundred to one thousand miles long. The Trail was short or long depending on what route you took and how much you zig-zagged. The standard time it took a wagon train to travel the Trail was anywhere from forty to seventy days.

On February 9, 1880, the railroad arrived in Santa Fe and the Trail became obsolete. Santa Fe was still a major hub of commerce but trade was now done by way of trains. The wagon caravans of the Santa Fe Trail were now too slow, too risky, and too expensive.

Santa Fe was now linked to both coasts by way of the Union Pacific, Southern Pacific, and Santa Fe Railroads. In 1881, Colorado and the Rocky Mountain areas were opened up to Santa Fe by way of the Denver Rio Grande Railroad.

All that now remains of the Santa Fe Railroad is the track spur that goes to Lamy. The Denver Rio Grande rails were torn up. Its only remaining track is the Cumbres-Toltec Railroad that now runs between Chama, New Mexico, and Antonito, Colorado.

Sadly, the Santa Fe Trail has not been that well preserved. However, a lot of the buildings in Santa Fe that stood during the Trail days are still in use today.

Southeast of Santa Fe, sections of the Trail can still be seen. Lore has it that the ruts found in the Amelia White Park are the wagon tracks that mark part of the old trail. Occasionally, a rainstorm or an excavation yields an old relic that belonged to a cowboy or merchant who traveled the Trail. [41]

A Train on the Santa Fe Railroad

THE HORSEMAN

The Santa Fe Trail was dangerous. There were bandits and hostile Indians that had to be outrun or fought. Depending on the time of the year, Santa Fe Trail riders or wagon caravans had to contend with muddy paths, flooded streams, scorching heat, wild fires, blizzards, and freezing temperatures.

Francois Xavier Aubry was the fastest rider on the Santa Fe Trail. Aubry was born outside Maskinonge, Quebec, Canada, in 1824. As a young man, Aubry arrived in Franklin, Missouri, and soon became a merchantman. Ladened with goods, Aubry would leave Franklin and arrive in Santa Fe in record time.

In Santa Fe, Aubry would sell the goods at a handsome profit then return to Missouri and do it all over again. Aubry developed a reputation for being the fastest rider on the Trail. Numerous times he broke the Trail's time record. Aubry's moniker was "Telegraph" because his speed on the Trail or other western paths was phenomenal.

Many times Aubry was wounded by Indians. Aubry was a smallish man who was fearless, and lore has it that Aubry was the first man to take a loaded wagon down the Santa Fe Trail during the winter.

Aubry also pioneered the Chihuahua Trail and the California Trail. His daring exploits were noted by his peers and valleys and cliffs were named after this intrepid man.

On September 12, 1848, Aubry left Santa Fe for Franklin, Missouri. He intended to break his Santa Fe Trail record one more time. This trip was special and legend has it that Aubry had bet anywhere from one thousand dollars to five thousand dollars that he would arrive at the end of the Trail in less than six days.

Even with everything going wrong, an exhausted Aubry arrived in Franklin, Missouri, in five days and sixteen hours. Aubry had averaged close to one hundred and forty miles per day, riding around the clock through storms and sunshine.

Aubry was so spent, that he had to be lifted out of his saddle and put to bed. The Santa Fe Trail speed record that Aubry set on horseback will probably stand forever.

On August 18, 1854, Aubry was murdered inside the Mercure Brothers store, located on the south side of the Plaza. Aubry had gotten into a fight with future Confederate Artillery Major, Richard Weightman, and was stabbed with a Bowie knife. Weightman died in combat in 1862 at the battle of Wilson Creek.

Aubry's exploits are not well known, but if there ever was a man who could ride as fast as the wind, it was Francois, Xavier Aubry. [42]

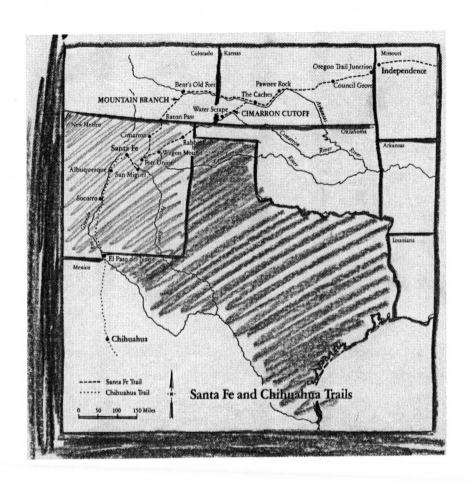

Santa Fe and Chihuahua Trails

A COMMON OCCURRENCE

On June 14, 1852, a soldier named James Augustus Bennet visited the La Fonda Hotel and wrote in his journal about what he witnessed. La Fonda in the 1800s was known by many names such as The Exchange Hotel or Hotel America, etc.

Bennet was seated in La Fonda's lobby when a cowboy came in and started shooting up the hotel. The cowboy said he was from Texas and was getting even for a friend of his who was killed. The cowboy shot a lawyer in the stomach and another man in the arm. The cowboy was then thrown into jail.

Later that night the cowboy from Texas was lynched and hung in the backyard of La Fonda. Violence in Santa Fe was a very ordinary thing in the days of the "Wild West." [43]

Wagon Train

SANTA FE'S MR. INDOMITABLE (A FORGOTTEN GOOD GUY!)

One of Santa Fe's good guys was Charlie Siringo. His autobiography was titled, *A Texas Cowboy or Fifteen Years on a Hurricane Deck of a Spanish Pony*. The book chronicled Siringo's early years as a cowboy in the Southwest.

Charles Angelo Siringo's life read as if it had been fashioned by a movie script writer. He was born in Matagora County, Texas, on February 7, 1855. Due to his father's death, by the age of twelve Siringo was working on cattle drives and sending his money home to his mother and siblings.

As a teen and a young man, Siringo worked all the major trails and cattle drives. Siringo became friends with Billy The Kid, Pat Garrett, and Bat Masterson, and worked for the notorious cattle boss, Shanghai Pierce.

Siringo witnessed many historic events such as the last big herd of plains bison and the building of the transcontinental railroad. Siringo was also involved in countless gunfights with hostile Indians, rustlers, and banditos.

At the age of thirty, Siringo settled down for a time in Caldwell, Kansas, and wrote his autobiography. He became a Western celebrity with the publication of his book. "Famous Person" status did not sit well with Siringo and he soon became restless and missed the adventurous life that he had found in the Southwest.

Siringo found a cure for his discontent by joining the Pinkerton Detective Agency. Once again he was involved in shootouts, trail rides, and murder investigations. Siringo's Pinkerton job took him from the eastern seaboard to Alaska. Siringo tracked down outlaws and infiltrated gangs by disguising himself as a desperado.

One of Siringo's greatest feats was bringing to justice "Big Bill Haywood," the dynamite murderer. Siringo was also a co-captain in the posse that hunted down Butch Cassidy and The Sundance Kid and led the posse that tracked the Wild Bunch.

In 1907, Siringo retired to Santa Fe and bought a ranch. Santa Fe's many Siringo roads are named after the man. New Mexico Governor William C. McDonald persuaded Siringo to come out of retirement, and in 1916 Siringo became an officer in the New Mexico Rangers.

Siringo, then in his sixties, was once again out on the trail fighting rustlers and banditos. He retired again in 1919 and wrote such books as *Lone Star Cowboy*, *The History of Billy the Kid*, and *Riata and Spurs*.

Charles Siringo died on October 18, 1928, in Altadena, California. Siringo was in California because his good friend, Hollywood Western star, William Hart, had talked Siringo into working in the film industry. Siringo spent the last years of his life working as an advisor on Western movies and writing movie scripts.

Siringo lived a life full of adventure and saw the West at its wildest. [44]

1920s Hollywood Camera

THE HONORABLE WILLIAM HENRY BONNEY, A.K.A. BILLY THE KID

The information surrounding Billy The Kid contradicts itself repeatedly. Here is what legend, lore, and facts say about the West's most notorious outlaw.

Billy The Kid was born William Henry Bonney in a Brooklyn slum of New York City on November 23, 1859. The Kid's mother was Katherine Bonney, a destitute, starving Irish immigrant, who worked as a part-time prostitute. Katherine also gave birth to another son named Joseph.

Katherine Bonney was attractive and had a sense of humor. She met and married Michael McCarty in New York City during the Civil War. McCarty was a wounded Yankee soldier who had been mustered out of the Union army.

The Kid at this stage of his life went by his middle name, Henry. With the marriage of his mother, he started going by his stepfather's last name, McCarty. The Kid was a quick learner and had a sense of humor. He also developed a talent for singing songs in a tenor voice.

The McCarty family left New York City and moved West in 1865 to seek a better life for themselves. In 1868, depending on the tale, Michael McCarty became ill and died. Alone again, either in Indianapolis, Indiana, or in Coffeyville, Kansas, depending on the story, Katherine, with few prospects, worked at all kinds of jobs to keep herself and her sons from starving.

It's possible that after the death of Michael McCarty, Katherine moved herself and her children back to New York City. Either in New York City or in Indianapolis, Indiana, Katherine met William Atrim, who was also a Civil War veteran. Katherine fell in love and she and her two boys began living with William Atrim.

William Atrim worked all kinds of jobs, from bartender to carpenter to farmer. To better their lot in life, William Atrim moved his new family to wherever there was employment.

The Atrim family lived all over the United States, from mining camps in the Rockies to New Orleans. In 1871, the Atrim family moved to Santa Fe, New Mexico.

William and Katherine Atrim worked odd jobs in Santa Fe, from running a boarding house to washing laundry. The Kid worked at La Fonda Hotel as a dishwasher and learned to speak Spanish fluently.

On March 1, 1873, Katherine married William Atrim at the First Presbyterian Church at 208 Grant Street. The church is still in existence. By getting married, Katherine was now considered an honest woman. If you cohabited outside of marriage during that era you were considered a fallen soul.

The First Presbyterian Church's marriage recordbook has inscribed in it The Kid's signature as Henry McCarty, as a witness to the marriage of William and Katherine Atrim. Joseph McCarty, The Kid's brother, also signed in as a witness.

In 1874, the Atrims moved to Silver City, New Mexico, and William Atrim and his stepson Joseph worked in the mountains as prospectors. The Kid went to school and helped his mother run a boarding house.

Legend has it that The Kid first got into big trouble outside a general store. A nameless man kept calling his mother a whore. The Kid killed the man with a single shot. Many New Mexico towns allege that this gunfight happened on their main street.

The Kid went to school in Silver City and was not a problem student. He was known for his love of dancing and singing. Katherine died of tuberculosis on September 16, 1874. Lore has it that at the death of his mother, William Henry McCarty became known as Billy The Kid or just plain, The Kid.

The Kid stayed in Silver City and waited tables at the Star Hotel. His brother and stepfather lived at Chloride Flat, where they continued to prospect. The Kid got into trouble in September of 1875 for ditching school and for hiding clothes in his room that "Sombrero Jack" had stolen from a Chinese laundry. The Kid was thrown into jail where he promptly escaped and headed out to Arizona.

In Arizona The Kid worked as a teamster and at different ranches as a saddle tramp. During this time in Arizona, The Kid perfected his shooting skills, fast draw, and became the fastest gun in the West. The Kid got into trouble again on August 17, 1877, when he refused to be bullied anymore by a blacksmith by the name of Frank P. "Windy" Cahill.

Cahill, who was an adult, called The Kid a pimp and threw hot grease at him. After this incident, The Kid called Cahill out, the two men met in the open, and a fair fight ensued. Cahill and The Kid went for their guns; Cahill died from a single shot.

The Kid was arrested and thrown into jail in Pima County, Arizona, whereupon he escaped by throwing salt into the jail guard's eye. The Kid rode into Mexico, and the posse that chased after him broke off its pursuit once it reached the Mexican border. The Kid resurfaced back in the United States in October of 1877, in Lincoln, New Mexico.

The Kid was taken in by Englishman rancher John Tunstall. At this point in time The Kid went back to his given name of William Henry Bonney but everybody else called him Billy The Kid or The Kid.

During the time between The Kid's escape into Mexico and his resurfacing in Lincoln County, myth and legend becomes very confused. Lore has it that during this time span, The Kid was befriended by and fought against different Indian tribes in the Southwest.

At Tunstall's ranch, The Kid found a home. The manor resembled the French Foreign Legion, in that Tunstall asked no questions about a person's past. All Tunstall asked from his workers was loyalty, which he got.

Unfortunately for The Kid, rancher Tunstall was involved in a mercantile rivalry in Lincoln County with the Murphy-Dolan faction. Tunstall was assassinated by gunmen employed by the Murphy-Dolan syndicate on February 28, 1878. This murder sparked the start of the Lincoln County War.

The Kid rode with ex-Tunstall employees, who were known as regulators. The name derives from when this group of cowboys had been sworn in as deputies. The regulators went on to fight it out with the men who backed the Murphy-Dolan syndicate.

The Kid fought with just about everybody who had a hand in the Tunstall murder or who had not been on Tunstall's side. The Kid took on gunmen, lawmen, bandits, or bounty hunters. Between battles, The Kid partook in cattle rustling.

From 1878 until his death in July of 1881, The Kid's reputation and popularity grew. The Kid became a cult hero that could be likened to what Elvis Presley was to the United States in the 1950s.

The Kid supposedly killed twenty-one men and lived a charmed life. No matter what the odds, The Kid could not be killed by typical gunfight means. The Kid was known to be likable and a songster, his favorite tunes being "Turkey in the Straw" and "Over the River."

Charlie Siringo, who lived in Santa Fe, was pals with The Kid. Siringo said, "The Kid was an excellent dancer and singer and had a girlfriend in every cantina and town." This may explain the fact or myth, that The Kid broke out of the Lincoln County jail by having one of his lady friends smuggle a key or pistol, depending on the story, into the jail in a tortilla or pie.

The Kid was captured at Stinking Springs, New Mexico, in November of 1880. The Kid was then transported in late December to Santa Fe and held at the city jail.

In Santa Fe, as a young teen living with his family, The Kid had been very well liked. As a captured outlaw, The Kid once again became a favorite of Santa Fe. The Kid was visited by locals, old friends, and by newspaper reporters. The Kid was described as being five feet seven inches tall with light hair, fair skin, slight build, and clear blue eyes.

While in Santa Fe, The Kid behaved himself and did not try to escape. By his word of honor, he was given parole, and entertained a large crowd of Santa Feans with his gunplay outside the city jail. The Kid was handed a pistol and many boxes of bullets, and he dazzled the deputies and locals with his trick shots and marksmanship.

The Kid shot bottles and objects thrown into the air. After the exhibition, The Kid smiled and went back to jail, not breaking his parole.

The Kid was then sent to Lincoln, New Mexico, where he again escaped from jail. The Kid was killed in Fort Sumner, New Mexico, on July 14, 1881, when he was shot down by his old friend, Pat Floyd Garrett, who was now the sheriff of Lincoln County. Lore has it that The Kid was shot in a dark room, and one account has The Kid being unarmed.

Garrett collected the reward for The Kid's death, and his name became infamous as the man who gunned down the West's most notorious outlaw. Garrett, who had lived in Santa Fe before he became sheriff of Lincoln County, was known to Santa Feans as Juan Largo which means Long John. Garrett was over six feet, four inches tall.

Garrett went on to make good money as an author, rancher, and Federal Customs Collector for the City of El Paso. Unfortunately, Garrett drank and gambled his money away. On February 29, 1908, he was murdered by a shot to the back of the head by Wayne Brazel in Las Cruces, New Mexico. [45]

Billy the Kid

YOU CAN'T BEAT THE PERCENTAGES

The legend, facts, and lore concerning Gertrudis Barcelo, who went by the nickname of Tules, is similar to that of Billy The Kid, in that dates and tales are not clear and stories contradict each other. What is fact is that from 1835 until her death in 1852, Tules was Santa Fe's most notorious and wealthiest woman.

Tules, who was sometimes referred to as La Tules or Doña Tules, ran the finest casino and bordello in the Southwest. Her den of iniquity was more than likely located where the Eldorado Hotel now stands, at 309 West San Francisco. Many people believe that Tules' casino and bordello was located off Burro Alley.

Before the Eldorado Hotel was built, the property that it was to be constructed on was occupied by a lumber yard. As the lumber yard was demolished to make way for the hotel, construction workers found the artifacts and foundations of a casino and bordello.

Throughout Santa Fe's "Wild West" era, Sandoval Street divided the proper part of town from the red light areas. Tules' casino and bordello was on the west side of Sandoval Street.

The casino and bordello was elaborate with fine cuisine, glass mirrors, carpet, billiard tables, magnificent chandeliers, and beautiful prostitutes.

In her prime, Tules was a ravishing raven-haired beauty. Many places claim to be her birth place: Spain, Mexico, Taos, etc. It is very probable that Tules was born in Spain and came to the Santa Fe area as a teenager. Her father was a card dealer and gambler, and he practiced his trade in Spain, Havana, New Orleans, Vera Cruz, and Mexico City. In the Mexican state of Sonora, Tules' father died or was murdered. Legend has it he was killed in a card game.

As a teenager, Tules became the wife of a Mexican lieutenant and lived in the Taos area. According to lore, her husband was soon killed. Tules, destitute and alone in Taos, was forced into or found work as a harlot. Legend has it Tules was married off to the cavalryman so that her mother and sister would have a small bounty to subsist on while living in Mexico. The Barcelo family was penniless after the father's death.

Seeing an opportunity and not liking her life in Taos, Tules moved or ran away to the mining camps south of Santa Fe and was soon running card games for high stakes. Tules then moved to Santa Fe and married a very elderly Manuel Cisneros. Tules gave birth to two sons, but both died as infants. What became of her husband is not clear.

In the 1830s, Tules opened her own casino and bordello in Santa Fe and proceeded to make a fortune. She was known for the great amounts of jewelry that she wore and her habit of smoking cigars. By the 1840s, Tules was thought to have become the richest woman in the West.

Tules did not come into her fortune by pure luck; she was a smart, literate woman, and she provided palatial comfort to those who could afford it. In an area of the world where creature comforts were hard to come by, Tules' house of ill repute and casino was an oasis of temptation and cleanliness.

For vacation and business purposes, Tules traveled back and forth between Mexico and Santa Fe. During one of these trips, she brought her mother and sister to Santa Fe to live with her and share her fortune.

Santa Fe from 1821 to 1846 was part of Mexico. During this time the authorities in Mexico City would select who would govern New Mexico and Santa Fe. Manuel Armijo, because of his wealth and strong political connections, was chosen many times to hold that post.

Armijo was a corrupt, cowardly, obese man, who lived opulently at the Palace of the Governors. Lore has it that Tules became Armijo's mistress. She did this not out of love but for business considerations. Tules knew that Armijo could cause all kinds of problems by leveling high duty fees on merchant convoys that came down the Santa Fe Trail.

Tules satisfied Armijo with her bribes and passion. In return, Armijo kept the Santa Fe Trail open and duty fees were kept in check. Accordingly, more monies poured into Santa Fe and this led to more wealth flooding into Tules' casino and bordello.

On May 13, 1846, the United States declared war on Mexico. That summer American troops advanced on Santa Fe. Governor Armijo assembled an army of Mexican regulars and Santa Fe Militia. This force of three thousand men were made ready for engagement.

The battle plan called for the American army to be stopped fifteen miles southeast of Santa Fe at the Cañoncito, Apache Ridge, and Apache Canyon areas. However, Armijo lost his nerve and fled with his personal bodyguard to Chihuahua, Mexico.

One tale has it that Armijo was bribed. In any case, once the army of Mexican regulars and Santa Fe Militia learned of its leader's cowardice, it surrendered to the Americans rather than fight for such a despicable man. On August 18, 1846, American soldiers entered Santa Fe. The conquest of Santa Fe was bloodless.

Brigadier General Stephen Kearny, who is sometimes erroneously listed as Colonel Kearney, ruled the area by military government. Some of the leading men of Santa Fe were not happy with being Americans, and a revolt was plotted.

The conspirators were led by Colonel Diego Archuleta and Tomas Ortiz. Tules found out about the rebellion either through pillow talk or from a prostitute who worked for her. Another tale has it that the revolt was planned in one of the casino-bordello's private rooms, and Tules spied on the goings on.

However it happened, Tules knew who would lead the insurrection and what the plans of action were. Tules concluded that at the end of the revolt, the Americans would be victorious but not after both sides suffered casualties. Tules also reasoned that her businesses could be hurt financially and perhaps destroyed during the fighting. With the idea of making profit and saving lives, Tules pitched her lot in with the Americans.

Tules informed the American authorities what was planned and who was involved. The American forces under the command of Colonel Sterling Price arrested the vast majority of leaders who were going to guide the revolt.

The uprising was thwarted before it ever got started, and from that point on Santa Fe remained a peaceful town as far as the American occupation was concerned. In retrospect, the conspirators were played like a drum by the highly intelligent and ruthless Tules.

A corollary to these stories of Tules being Santa Fe's version of "Mata Hari" is that Tules did not die of natural causes in 1852, but from being poisoned. Lore has it that her murder was a retribution for her collaboration with the Americans.

For all that, the Mexican–American War ended with the July 4, 1848, signing of the Hidalgo y Guadalupe Treaty. Both sides pledged peace and Mexico ceded their part of the Southwest and Santa Fe to the United States.

Now that Santa Fe was part of the United States, the city was free of customs duties or bribes to be paid. Trade on the Santa Fe Trail became a bull market. As the adage goes, profits were tossed up into the air by the horns of the bulls. Tules' bordello and casino reached its zenith in revenues when Santa Fe became part of the United States.

By 1850, Tules had become one of the wealthiest women in the United States. Tules did not hoard her fortune. Supposedly, she gave money to charity, public works, and those in need.

On January 17, 1852, Tules died and was buried under what is now the right wing of Saint Francis Cathedral. Tules, through her will, took care of her family, friends, and charities. Tules was buried with the highest honors the Catholic Church could give and it made a handsome profit on Tules' burial.

Tules' estate was charged a thousand dollars for having the Archbishop commemorate over the burial. The Church was also given fifty dollars for each time the procession that carried Tules' coffin was stopped by grieving individuals who tossed flowers or uttered prayers.

One thing is certain, Tules was one of the shrewdest women to ever live in Santa Fe. From humble origins she built a money machine out of vice.

Tules was a capitalist who played the percentages and was more than a match for the men who she gambled with, enticed, or bamboozled. Tules was the epitome of the rags to riches story. She is Santa Fe's version of Evita Peron. 46

Courtesan Employed by Doña Tules

ANOTHER COMMON OCCURRENCE

During the "Wild West" days, Santa Fe was the scene of many violent events. Gunplay and death were so common that the local newspapers would just give a date and minimal facts.

For example, the *Santa Fe Gazette* on September 29, 1866, reported that a person was killed and many were wounded in a shootout at the southwest corner of the Plaza. No other details were divulged, for shootings and death were just too standard an event for it to be considered big news in Santa Fe. [47]

HE LOST HIS HEAD

Thomas "Black Jack" Ketchum was a bear of a man who resembled an overweight professional wrestler. Black Jack was born in San Saba County, Texas, on October 31, 1863. Black Jack was not the most successful outlaw the West ever saw. His notoriety or immortality was due to how he died.

Black Jack and his brother Sam Ketchum rode with such gangs as the "Wild Bunch" and the "Hole In The Wall Gang." In New Mexico the Ketchums ran their own gang, which robbed trains, stage coaches, and post offices.

Black Jack and his gang hid out somewhere between Cerrillos and Santa Fe. It's of interest that their hideaway, be it a cave, a dilapidated shack, or canyon overhang, has never been found. It's highly unlikely that there is any buried treasure at the hideout because Black Jack and his gang could shoot it out but they never made the big score.

Luck and Black Jack were always strangers, and that bad fortune seemed to rub off on the men who rode in the Ketchum gang because Black Jack's henchmen were shot dead, hung, or died in prison.

While robbing the Santa Fe Railroad, Black Jack was badly wounded. Near death, the burly outlaw was taken by his gang to the Palace Hotel in Cerrillos. The outlaws forced a doctor who was staying at the hotel to attend to Black Jack's gunshot wound, and at gunpoint the doctor saved Black Jack's life.

The Palace Hotel of Cerrillos burned down in 1968, but prior to that it was a tourist stop. Vacationers would go to the hotel and take snapshots while standing next to the large faded blood puddle on the hotel's floor. The timeworn blood stain marked the spot where Black Jack was cut open and his wound cauterized.

Things went from bad to worse for Black Jack. His brother Sam was wounded in a gun battle with a posse and then captured on July 1, 1899. Sam Ketchum was thrown into the Santa Fe prison where he died from blood poisoning on July 24, 1899.

The Santa Fe prison at that time was located at the present-day intersection of Saint Francis Drive and Cordova Road. (Sam Ketchum's body was buried in the prison cemetery which by best estimate is now under Saint Francis Drive.)

Black Jack moved on to other areas and was wounded again in a holdup attempt in northeast New Mexico and captured. Black Jack was then tried for his crimes and found guilty. His sentence was death by hanging.

On April 26, 1901, at 1:21 P.M. in Clayton, New Mexico, Black Jack Ketchum was hung. Due to Black Jack's heavy weight and the inexperience of the hangman (the rope was not the right length for the drop), Black Jack was decapitated during the hanging.

On the gallows, Black Jack shook hands with his executioners and his last words were, "Let er rip." Odd words for a man who was decapitated during the hanging. Hours before his death, Black Jack confessed to his crimes, then changed his mind and said that he was not Black Jack Ketchum. He furthermore mentioned that "death was preferable to life in prison." Black Jack also told his lawyer to tell Harrington, the man who had wounded Ketchum in the hold-up, that he would see him in Hell for breakfast.

Black Jack wrote a final letter to his lawyer: "My advice to the boys of the country is not to steal horses or sheep but either rob a train or a bank. When you get to be an outlaw and every man who comes in your way, kill him. Spare him no mercy, for he will show you none." Black Jack Ketchum was a black-hearted man to the very end. [48]

Black Jack Ketchum

NEW MEXICO INVADED
AND THE GETTYSBURG
OF THE WEST

The battle of Glorieta was fought fifteen miles to the southeast of Santa Fe. This battle is called the Gettysburg of the West because it was the turning point for the Confederacy's Civil War fortunes in the West.

In 1862, a Confederate Army lead by General Henry Sibley marched from Texas into New Mexico following the Rio Grande River. The Confederate Army's goal was to capture New Mexico and Colorado. The rich mineral fields of Colorado were the economic objective of the campaign.

Sibley had been an army officer stationed in New Mexico and knew the territory well. When hostilities broke out between the North and the South, Sibley resigned his army commission and took up arms for the Confederacy.

Sibley's battalions were staffed with fine junior officers who commanded well-trained soldiers. The Confederate cadre consisted mainly of Texicans who had combat experience from fighting in the Comanche wars.

The Union forces in New Mexico were made up of regulars who garrisoned Western forts and volunteer units. The Union forces engaged the Confederates in many skirmishes and small battles in southern and central New Mexico. In these engagements, after hard fighting, the Confederates were victorious.

The Confederates' victories enabled them to occupy Mesilla, Socorro, and Albuquerque. On March 7, 1862, the Confederate army occupied Santa Fe and the Stars and Bars battle flag flew over the Palace of the Governors.

The Confederates refitted quickly in Santa Fe and then marched upon the Union army that occupied the battle line at Glorieta Pass. The Union army was commanded by Colonel John Slough. From March 26 through March 28, both Union and Confederate armies fought for control of the pass.

At the end of the long, confusing, bloody battle, the Confederates held the pass but it was a hollow victory. During the battle a Union calvary unit had raided the Confederate supply train and destroyed it.

The destruction of the Confederate army's supply column was complete. Sixty-four supply wagons were torched and eleven hundred pack mules were destroyed.

The loss of this supply column meant that the Confederate army could not march with ammunition or food stores. Even though the Confederate forces had beaten the Union forces at Glorieta, the Confederates were forced to retreat back to Santa Fe.

If this supply column had not been smashed, the victorious Confederate Army would have marched on Fort Union in Las Vegas, New Mexico. If victorious at Fort Union, the Confederate Army would have then marched into Colorado.

In Santa Fe, the Confederates refitted again, whereupon General Sibley decided that his army could not live off the land and ordered his army to retreat back to Texas. This was a mistake. Spring was near and the land would be bountiful, but Sibley's judgment had become clouded because of his bouts with alcoholism.

Before the battle of Glorieta, the Confederate forces had fought a desperate battle with Union troops at Valverde in central New Mexico. The hard-won Confederate victory had rocked Sibley's confidence. From that point on, Sibley hit the bottle regularly and his strategic clarity was clouded.

In Sibley's defense of his general retreat order, a Union army was approaching New Mexico from California. This Union army's objective was to cut off the Confederate army in New Mexico and smash it.

Sibley's forces would have been outnumbered and would have had very little in supplies. Nevertheless, the Confederates had defeated everything that had been thrown against them.

On April 11, 1862, the Confederate Army evacuated Santa Fe and began their retreat to the Southeast. On April 12, 1862, Union forces reoccupied Santa Fe and once again "Old Glory" flew over the Palace of the Governors.

The absence of a second Confederate invasion into New Mexico was a major blunder. If the mineral fields of Colorado had been controlled by the Confederacy, it is conceivable that this captured wealth could have brought European countries into the Civil War on the Confederacy's side through concessions and bribes.

During the Civil War, Mexico was occupied by French Foreign Legion troops under the command of Emperor Maximilian. If France or other European powers had entered into the war on the Confederacy's side, the outcome of the Civil War would have been very different. At any rate, the captured mineral wealth of Colorado would have bought the outgunned Confederacy the weaponry that it desperately needed by way of European arm merchants.

Tactically, the Battle of Glorieta was a Confederate victory, for they had driven the Union forces from the pass. Strategically, the battle was a smashing Union victory, because the Confederates lost their impetus for the offensive and retreated, after claiming the battlefield.

The Glorieta battlefield is now a largely overgrown area. There are a few markers in the Glorieta-Pecos-Pigeon Ranch areas that mark the combat spots of the Gettysburg of the West. If you are a Civil War buff, the Glorieta battlefield area is a must-see. [49]

Colt Revolver

THE GUNFIGHTERS WHO COULDN'T SHOOT STRAIGHT

The Plaza was the scene of a drunken shootout on June 20, 1876. Two friends, Van Ness Smith and Joe Stinson, who made their living as gamblers, got into a drunken argument at a downtown bar and decided to meet in the Plaza and shoot it out.

Stinson, with a colt revolver, stood in the central area of the Plaza near the obelisk monument. Smith, with a lever action Winchester rifle, stood near the east end of the Plaza. Both men fired their weapons simultaneously, but most of their shots went wild.

Lore has it that Smith managed to hit the Plaza obelisk a few times on its east face. Bullet scars can be seen on that side of the monument. There have been many gun fights and hell-raising episodes on the Plaza before and after this gunfight. With that in mind, the obelisk's bullet scars may or may not be the result of Smith's scattered shots. Once the two drunks had shot off all their bullets, the gunfight ended.

Both men were more than likely too inebriated to reload their weapons. When the two gamblers had sobered up, fable has it that the two trigger men went back to being best pals. The astonishing thing about this shootout is that nobody on the Plaza was hit by any of the wild shots that these two men fired. [50]

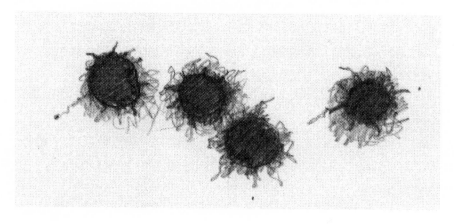

Bullet Holes

SHOWDOWN AT LA FONDA

On the afternoon of December 15, 1867, La Fonda lobby was the scene of a classic Western showdown. Chief Justice John Slough, thirty-eight, and William Logan Rynerson, thirty-nine, called each other out and dueled.

Slough was a big strong man who weighed over two hundred pounds and stood six feet tall. He was known for his quick temper, biting tongue, and bully tactics.

Slough was born in Cincinnati, Ohio, and was a member of the Ohio legislature. Slough's temperament momentarily derailed his political career, when he was expelled from the Ohio assembly for striking a fellow legislator.

In New Mexico during the Civil War, Slough commanded the Union army at the battle of Glorieta. The three-day battle was fought over a mountain pass. The Union companies under Slough were mauled and driven off the ground that they fought to defend.

The Confederate army that had defeated Slough's army, was forced to retreat being that its supply column was destroyed by a Union calvary squadron. Slough, ever the politician, took credit for the Union victory at Glorieta.

With a promotion, Slough was sent to the Maryland and Virginia theaters of the Civil War. Slough reaped the rewards of victory brought to him by his more capable subordinates in the Shenandoah Campaign.

As the war went on, Slough became a political strongman in Washington. He was assigned to be the Military Governor of Alexandria, Virginia, where he handled all the court martial cases. When President Abraham Lincoln was assassinated, Slough was one of the President's pall bearers.

With the Civil War over, Slough came back to New Mexico and launched himself into New Mexican politics and soon held great sway in the New Mexico Legislature.

Rynerson, Slough's rival, was a tall, strong and corrupt man. He was born in Kentucky and during the Civil War he had attained the rank of colonel while stationed in the Southwest. Rynerson, like Slough, had limited military skills and did not distinguish himself during the Confederate army's invasion of New Mexico.

After the Civil War, Rynerson won election to the New Mexico Legislature and he clashed with Slough. During the 1867 legislative session, he had Slough censured.

The feud between Rynerson and Slough grew and grew. On December 14, 1867, the day before the showdown at La Fonda, Slough told the legislators in Santa Fe that Rynerson was "a thief in the army, a thief out of the army and is now a coward and a son-of-a-bitch."

The next day, December 15, Slough walked into the La Fonda lobby on his way to play billiards and grab a drink at the bar. Rynerson, who was staying at La Fonda, happened to be in the lobby and spotted him.

Rynerson confronted Slough and demanded that the foul words that had beseeched his honor be taken back. Heated words were exchanged and Slough reached for his pocketed Derringer pistol. Rynerson instantly pulled out his Colt revolver and shot Slough.

Slough died within the hour. Depending on the story, Slough passed on either in the La Fonda lobby or what is now La Fonda's Plazuela Restaurant. It's of note that in 1867, La Fonda was called The Exchange Hotel.

Upon Slough's death, Rynerson was arrested, put on trial, and found not guilty. The verdict was justifiable homicide, for Rynerson was defending his life.

With Slough's death, Rynerson acquired more political power and went on to become a District Attorney and, in time, became the legal hatchet man for the Dolan-Murphy cabal in Lincoln County.

Rynerson hired the gunmen that killed English rancher John Tunstall of Lincoln County. That murder, which occurred on February 28, 1878, triggered the start of the Lincoln County War.

After Tunstall's assassination, Rynerson hired the John Kinney gang and this group of men waged a war against Billy The Kid and the Tunstall partisans. In 1880, Rynerson served as Billy The Kid's prosecuting attorney in the case of Sheriff William Brady's murder.

The showdown in the La Fonda lobby on December 15 altered history. If Rynerson had not survived the duel, would the Lincoln County War have been so bloody? Would it have started? Without the Lincoln County War, would Billy The Kid have made history and become the legend that he is today?

If Slough had won the duel with Rynerson, it is very likely that in the near future of the then 1870s, Slough would have become governor of New Mexico. Would Slough's ambition have taken him to the White House? [51]

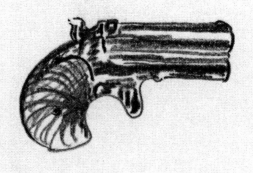

Derringer Pistol

THE WORDSMITH

Lew Wallace, author of *Ben Hur*, was Governor of New Mexico from 1878 to 1881. During his term as governor, Wallace wrote the novel while residing at the Palace of the Governors. His bedroom/study, which is sometimes called the Ben Hur Room, can be seen today when one tours the museum.

Some other novels penned by Wallace were *The Fair God*, *Prince of India*, and *A Tale of The Conquest of Mexico*. Wallace was also an accomplished poet and painter.

Wallace was born in Indiana in 1827. He became a lawyer and served in the Civil War as a Union general. Wallace was blamed for the Union army's near catastrophic defeat at the Battle of Shiloh in 1862. He was accused of being too cautious with his troops and marching his army at too slow a pace.

The charges were basically unfounded, but Wallace was labeled as a bumbler. Wallace was a competent commander and later on he saved Washington, D.C., from the Confederate calvary offensive of 1864. Wallace's forces thoroughly defeated General Jubal Early's Confederates.

In 1878, Wallace was appointed governor of New Mexico by President Rutherford B. Hayes. Wallace was chosen to replace the corrupt Governor Samuel Axtell, who was a member of the "Santa Fe Ring." The Ring was a ruthless political machine that ruled New Mexico during it's "Wild West" days.

During Wallace's term as governor, Santa Fe was a rich frontier town that knew few limits. Wallace was appalled at what he saw when he first arrived. The town was a mecca for capitalism, violence, gambling, and sin.

Wallace slowly brought order to New Mexico and Santa Fe, but his main passion was writing, not governing. Upon completion of *Ben Hur*, neither Wallace nor anybody else could imagine that a modern classic had been written. Throughout the late 1800s and into the turn of the century, *Ben Hur* was a bestseller.

In the 1920s, *Ben Hur* was filmed and it became a silent film classic. It was re-filmed in the middle 1950s and became a modern masterpiece.

After completing his term as governor in Santa Fe, Wallace was appointed diplomat to the Ottoman Empire. Late in life Wallace became an inventor and had many of his devices patented.

Wallace died in 1905, a true Renaissance man. [52]

A MAN MISUNDERSTOOD

The Kit Carson Monument is located at the crossroads of Lincoln Avenue and South Federal Place. The obelisk monument was erected in 1885 by veterans of the Grand Army of the Republic. The words on the monument adequately sum up who Kit Carson was. The monument reads, "He Led the Way."

Kit Carson is either loathed or loved. It seems there is nothing ambivalent about this Western character. Those historians who hate him, claim that Carson was a racist and was the ruination of the Navajo people. Those who praise Carson say that he has been unjustly pilloried for what transpired after the Navajo War of 1863-1865.

If one goes by the Western standards of the 1800s, Carson was not as barbarous or brutal as other American commanders or Indian chiefs who fought in the West.

Be that as it may, here are the facts concerning Carson and the Navajo. In 1863 the United States declared war on the Navajo nation, and Kit Carson was put in command of the combat troops that engaged the Navajo.

Hopi, Zuni, Pueblo, and Ute Indian tribes allied with the American troops, and these different forces defeated the Navajo by laying waste to the Navajo's homeland. The campaign was similar to how the Union army defeated the Confederacy during the Civil War.

By the end of 1865, the Navajo had been defeated and its populace, estimated to be anywhere from eight thousand to fifteen thousand people, surrendered to the American army.

The Navajo sought out the American forces and surrendered to them rather than to the Zuni, Hopi, Pueblo, or Ute tribes that were warring against them. If the Navajo had surrendered to these other tribes, it is likely that the Navajo nation would have ceased to exist.

Upon the end of hostilities, the Navajo were marched from their homeland, which is in northwest New Mexico, to Bosque Redondo, which is near Fort Sumner in eastern New Mexico. The Navajo were separated into fifty-three groups and marched three hundred miles.

During these marches to Fort Sumner many young and old Navajo died due to the cold, lack of food, and sickness. The official record states that three hundred and sixty-seven Navajo died on this trek. More than likely there were many more fatalities because records do not agree on how many Navajo were incarcerated at Bosque Redondo. Nonetheless, if the American officers with rank had treated the Navajo as human beings rather than non-feeling enemies, this Navajo trek disaster could have been avoided.

What makes historians and people of today despise Carson is that he had a hand in conquering the Navajo nation. This conquest led to the Navajo's death march.

Carson's defenders claim that he had no authority over these marches and that all Carson did was to defeat a determined hostile enemy. After the campaign was over, other officers in the army engineered the Navajo's catastrophic march and confinement at Bosque Redondo. Who is right and who is wrong?

In 1868, the Navajo were released and sent back to their homeland.

As for what caused this war, the facts are as follows. The Navajo nation had continually raided New Mexico ranches, homesteads, and neighboring Indian settlements for decades. Livestock was stolen, and men, women, and children were killed or kept as slaves. Plain and simple, the Navajo waged war against Americans, Spaniards, Mexicans, and various other Indian tribes.

In the end, the Navajo were thoroughly defeated. Nonetheless, the long walk and the Navajo incarceration in dreadful conditions at Bosque Redondo cannot be justified. Was Carson responsible for this? It is debatable.

Kit Carson was born on December 24, 1809, and died in 1868. At the age of fourteen Carson was apprenticed to a saddle maker in Missouri. At age sixteen Carson ran away and ended up in Santa Fe after trekking down the Santa Fe Trail.

What Kit Carson accomplished in his life is impressive. He was an explorer, trapper, soldier, and family man. Carson fought for the Union (Grand Army of the Republic) during the Civil War and against hostile Indians. Carson was not a paper shuffler; he led his men through shot and shell. Carson wed three times; his first two wives were Indian, his third was Mexican. Carson also adopted and raised an Indian boy. Would a racist do this? Contemporaries of Carson wrote in their journals that Carson was a generous, brave, God-fearing man.

Not many people are written about in such glowing terms. Carson risked his life many times helping others. Carson was not despised or hated, he was loved and respected.

Seventeen years after Carson's death, five thousand people were on hand to honor his memory when the obelisk monument at Federal Place was dedicated.

Kit Carson

BAD LUCK PAULA!

Paula Angel, of Las Vegas, New Mexico, a seamstress (age nineteen, depending on the record), was the first and only woman ever hung in New Mexico. Paula was executed on April 26, 1861, in San Miguel County, which shares its border with Santa Fe County.

Where Paula was executed is not clear because the records only indicate that Paula was hung from a cottonwood tree that stood in a grassy field. Paula's crime was murder. In a fit of rage she stabbed to death her lover, Juan Miguel Martin. The argument that led to the death of Martin started over outraged virtue and broken promises.

Martin, age twenty-two, son of a wealthy Santa Fe family, seduced Paula and promised her many things. On March 23, 1861, Martin ended the affair that led to his death. Martin died by stiletto wound in Las Vegas, New Mexico, in a bar on Church Street.

Paula was arrested and then tried in court. The trial was a fast event and on March 28 the jury ruled that Paula was guilty of first degree murder. Death by hanging was the mandatory punishment.

The presiding judge was Kirby Benedict who stacked the case against Paula. Judge Benedict had instructed the jury to either find Paula guilty of first degree murder or not guilty. A crime of passion defense was negated by this instruction. Paula had killed her lover and that fact ruled out the verdict of not guilty. The jury was left with only one option, murder in the first degree.

A poetic ballad titled, "La Homicida de Pablita" tells of the event. Paula was confined to a jail cell in Las Vegas, New Mexico, and her days in jail were not pleasant. She was constantly tormented by Sheriff Antonio Herrera, who told her in detail how gruesome a death by hanging could be and how little time she had left.

On the day she was to be hung, Sheriff Herrera put Paula into the wagon that carried her coffin. Paula was teased and harangued to the very end. At the hanging tree, a great crowd estimated to be around 2,000 people had gathered to witness what had never been done before, the death of a woman by noosed rope.

The crowd was made up of Spanish-Mexican Americans, and their value system of that day opposed the idea of killing a woman with a noose. Overseeing the hanging was J.D. Sena from Santa Fe. He was a powerful politician. His instructions were to make sure Paula was executed, and that he did.

Sena came from a wealthy old Santa Fe family. Lore has it that Sena was reared at Sena Plaza, which is located at 125 East Palace Avenue. During Santa Fe's "Wild West days," Sena Plaza was a grand home. Today, it's a beautiful complex of stores, offices, and restaurants.

For some reason that is lost to history, it was deemed that Paula would be hung from a tree not from the gallows. Was this done out of maliciousness? Did Paula's personality or feminine beauty trigger jealousy or hatred from the officials? Some old timers surmise that Paula could not pay for her scaffold, so she was hung from a tree.

A person being hung from a tree dies slowly by strangulation. It's conceivable that a person can linger kicking away for air from one to twenty minutes. A tree hanging is a painful, bloody death.

Paula was placed in the back of a wagon and the noose placed around her neck. The crowd crossed themselves as Sheriff Herrera got into the driver's seat and whipped his horses forward. The crowd gasped and roared when they saw that Herrera and Sena had not tied Paula's arms behind her back. More than likely, Paula in her death struggle had managed to free her arms from the ropes that bound them. Paula was now kicking and holding onto the rope that was choking her.

Sheriff Herrera stopped his horses and ran to Paula who was kicking and heaving as she hung from the tree. He grabbed Paula's struggling torso and legs and yanked the suffocating woman downward.

The crowd had now seen enough and rushed to the struggling duo and threw Sheriff Herrera down and quickly lowered Paula to the ground.

The crowd yelled out that Paula was hanged, the sentence had been carried out. Others in the crowd said it was a sign from God that Paula was not supposed to be killed.

The unspoken rule in any hanging is, if the condemned person is able to cheat death, then that persons's life is spared. A broken rope or a bungled execution means life for the condemned.

Sena ordered that Paula be hung again until dead. He then ordered Sheriff Herrera's men to keep order over the crowd. If need be, they were to fire upon anyone or any group who tried to interfere with the hanging.

Paula was again placed in the wagon, but this time her arms were securely tied behind her back. The crowd rushed the wagon and scuffles broke out. Sena was bloodied but the rescue attempt was in vain. The wagon was again pulled from beneath Paula's feet. This time, "Bad Luck Paula" was successfully hung.

It's of note that Paula Angel was the first woman ever hung in the United States or in the Territorial United States. Mary Elizabeth Surrat is erroneously noted as the first woman to be hung in the United States.

Surrat was hung on July 7, 1865, in Washington, D.C., having been found guilty of being a conspirator in the assassination of President Abraham Lincoln. [54]

Tarnished Badge

THERE'S GOLD IN THEM THAR HILLS!

In 1828, gold fever hit Santa Fe. Lore has it that a sheepherder or mule skinner tending to his animals picked up a heavy yellow stone in the Ortiz Mountains which are twenty miles south of Santa Fe. This nameless man then had the heavy rock looked at while he was in Santa Fe and the stone was discovered to be pure gold. Word spread of this find and the gold rush was on.

The story is a nice fable, but who or what started the 1828 gold rush cannot be verified. The facts are that by the end of 1829 mining camps dotted the Ortiz Mountains and the area was honeycombed with mines.

The Ortiz Mountains gold rush preceded the California strikes by over twenty years. Historians claim that the 1848 gold rush was the first major gold discovery in what is now the western United States.

The historians are wrong. Spanish Colonial Santa Feans worked the Ortiz Mountains prior to the Indian revolt of 1680. The strike of

1828 was in essence a continuation of what the Spaniards had prospected for centuries earlier.

The 1828 rush ebbed as the gold yield in the worked areas decreased. New strikes were hit in 1839 and 1879 and all through the 1890s. The upshot was that new waves of prospectors came to the Ortiz Mountains via Santa Fe.

Today, a few high tech companies still work the old gold strike areas with state of the art rock crushing equipment. These companies have armed guards patrolling their mining areas and sightseeing on these lands is prohibited.

In spite of that, there is still plenty of unclaimed territory in and around the Ortiz Mountains that can be hiked. These areas are littered with spent mines and ruins of old digs. [55]

The Gold Rush

6

TALES OF SANTA FE: MODERN TIMES

LA FONDA

La Fonda in Spanish means the inn or tavern. It is alleged that La Fonda can trace its hotel heritage back to 1610. Since that year, there has always been a lodge at the corner of Shelby and San Francisco Streets. La Fonda during the "Wild West" days was known for its fine food, elegance, billiard tables, and shootouts.

Through the centuries, La Fonda has had many names, such as "The Exchange Hotel," "The U.S. Hotel," "The Fonda," "La Fonda Americana," etc. Through the centuries La Fonda has been the end of the trail meeting place for pioneers, businessmen, tourists, and celebrities.

Architecturally, La Fonda, with its Pueblo-like look, is one of the most beautiful hotels in the world. Some of La Fonda's guests have been Buffalo Bill, Salvador Dali, Tyrone Powers, and Zsa Zsa Gabor.

Errol Flynn rates as one of La Fonda's most troublesome guests. On Friday night, December 13, 1940, the movie, *Santa Fe Trail* was premiered at the Lensic Theater, located at 225 West San Francisco. Flynn, being the star of the film, was on hand for the world premier of the movie.

After the movie's spectacular showing, complete with wagon and horsemen outside the theater, Flynn went back to La Fonda and had too many margaritas. Inebriated, according to legend, Flynn started swinging from balcony to balcony by way of rope and curtains, pretending he was Robin Hood and welcoming the La Fonda guests to Sherwood Forest as he balanced on different banisters. Flynn had previously played the Robin Hood character in a 1938 film. Fencing with an imaginary Sir Guy of Gisbourne and leaping from balconies, Flynn spent a good part of the night thinking he was back on a Hollywood sound stage as he delivered lines from that swashbuckler epic.

La Fonda is steeped in history. If you get a chance, take a stroll through the hotel and enjoy its splendor. There is nothing else like it in the world. [56]

La Fonda, The Inn at the End of the Santa Fe Trail

THE BRICKS

The Plaza was refurbished in the spring and summer of 1974. The bricks that made up the road and sidewalks of the Plaza were torn up and replaced with four hundred twenty-five thousand new bricks. The old Plaza bricks were left in piles and given away to anybody who wanted them. If those bricks could only talk. Imagine how much history they had witnessed over the years. [57]

THE TOWN SQUARE

The Conquistadors, under the command of Pedro de Peralta, built the Plaza in 1610 when they founded Santa Fe. De Peralta's men followed the orders of King Philip II's 1573 Laws of the Indies.

The edict read that every Spanish city must have a starting point, that being the center of the town. The Plaza was designed for military, religious, and commercial functions. The Plaza's rich history includes proclamations, battles, gunfights, markets, parades, marriages, and riots. Almost anything of public or private nature has happened at the Plaza.

The Santa Fe Trail ended at the southeast corner of the Plaza. From 1821 to 1880, American merchantmen journeyed from Missouri to Santa Fe in wagons. Upon arriving in the Plaza, the traders unloaded and sold their items for a handsome profit.

The Plaza was also the starting point of other famous western trails. The Escalante Trail which goes to Taos started at the Plaza. Also the Camino Real, which is known as the Royal Road or Chihuahua Trail, started at the Plaza.

The Camino Real journeyed south to Albuquerque, then through La Mesilla, Chihuahua, Mexico City, and terminated at the Mexican Gulf port city of Vera Cruz. The Plaza is one of the most unique places in all the world. For close to four hundred years it has been the focal point for commerce and all types of gathering. The Plaza is one of the world's true crossroads. [58]

GIVE TILL IT HURTS

The Battle of Glorieta was fought southeast of Santa Fe in 1862. This Civil War battle has been termed the Gettysburg of the West. Two cannons that were used in that battle were on display in the Plaza up until October 15, 1942.

During World War II, American towns gave old steel products to American war industrial plants. In turn the plants would melt down the metal and reform the steel into modern fighting implements that would be used against America's World War II enemies.

Towns across America would mobilize for iron or tin drives, and old metal would be collected at a depot and then shipped off to the nearest war factory. In 1942, Santa Fe's city council voted to give the Plaza's two civil war cannons to the local Federal authorities who were running the metal collection drive in Santa Fe.

The cannons along with other Santa Fe metal products were gathered and sent to a military plant to be melted down.

Albuquerque's city council showed more foresight than Santa Fe officials. Albuquerque did contribute to the scrap iron drive. However, Albuquerque's two civil war cannons were not sent off to some furnace. The city council of Albuquerque refused to let go of its two captured Rebel cannons.

Today, Albuquerque's Confederate cannons are on display in Albuquerque's Museum of History. One wishes that Santa Fe's cannons were still intact and on display. [59]

THE OBELISK

In the center of the Plaza is a monument that honors the soldiers who fell in battle during the Civil War and Indian wars. The monument was built in 1867. The obelisk has a few gun shot scars on it, the results of the many gunfights that took place on the Plaza during Santa Fe's "Wild West" days.

A time capsule was buried somewhere in the Plaza during the laying of the cornerstone for the monument in 1867. It was thought that the capsule was buried under or near the monument. In 1967, at the centennial of the obelisk, the sealed box was to be dug up. Unfortunately, the directions from 1867 were wrong, because the time capsule was not found. Many attempts have been made to find the sealed box but all have met with failure. The capsule contained documents and coins. [60]

TICK TOCK

The Spitz clock, located at the corner of Palace and Lincoln Avenues, has been a Santa Fe landmark since 1881. There have been three Spitz clocks. Lore has it that the first clock did not run. The second clock was posted in 1900 but was destroyed in 1915 when a truck ran into it. The third clock has been in Santa Fe since 1916, having been bought second hand in Kansas City.

The third clock was a great bargain for that second hand time piece has been keeping time for more than a lifetime. While standing by the Spitz clock, you can hear the gears of that time piece clicking and meshing. The clock was built by the Howard Watch & Clock Company of Boston over a century ago. Fortunately, this beautiful timepiece was not melted for scrap during World War II like the Plaza's Civil War cannon. [61]

The Spitz Clock

THE CATRON BLOCK

The beautiful two story Catron Building on the east side of the Plaza was completed in 1891 by Thomas Catron, a Republican politician, businessman, and lawyer. It is claimed that the Catron Building was the first structure in Santa Fe to have an elevator.

Thomas Catron ran his law practice out of his second story office that looked down upon the Plaza and the Palace of the Governors. Catron's personal law library, which was on the second floor, was reputed to be the biggest collection of law books west of the Mississippi. Today, as it was in the 1890s, the first floor of the Catron Building consists of retail shops. [62]

PALACE OF THE GOVERNORS

The Palace of the Governors, on the north side of the Plaza, was built by Spanish Conquistadors in 1610. Initially the Palace was designed to be a fortress government building. The old Palace of the Governors extended from the Plaza to Marcy Street. The building is a mere shell of its former self.

Two medieval-like towers (Torreones) flanked the east and west sides of the Palace of the Governors. None of the old battlements exist. As the town and area became tame, the stone and blocks of these fortifications were used to build houses and roadways.

The outside rectangular walls that house the Palace of the Governors give one an idea of how massive the old fortress was. These walls are at least three feet thick. Housed inside this building were offices, private apartments, military barracks, a chapel, cells, court, arsenal, and the regal governor's quarters.

The Palace of the Governors is the oldest continuously occupied government building in the United States. Santa Fe has been ruled by Spain, Mexico, Pueblo Indians, Confederate States of America, and the

United States of America. No matter who controlled New Mexico, that governing power used the Palace of the Governors as their headquarters from 1610 to 1885.

A new capitol building was built in 1885, and in 1909 the Palace of the Governors became a museum. This old, magnificent building predates the Pilgrims landing at Plymouth Rock by many years. [63]

THE UNCOMPLETED BUILDING

Saint Francis Cathedral is named after the patron saint of Santa Fe. The cathedral is the third church to occupy that site. The first church was built between 1626 and 1629. It was destroyed during the Indian Revolt of 1680. The second church was built after the reconquest in 1714. The present day cathedral was constructed between 1869 and 1886. However, sources do not agree on the 1800s dates.

When construction started on the church, Santa Fe did not have many Catholic masons. Archbishop Lamy solved that problem by recruiting masons from Italy and France to come to Santa Fe and work on his brainchild.

The cathedral was originally designed to be much larger and grander. The two front towers were supposed to be three stories taller and be crowned with spires. Due to money problems, the cathedral was finished with a design that was operational but not as elegant as planned.

The large blocks of stone on top of the north tower give evidence to the planned construction of the tower's next level. It is alleged that the cathedral was designed to be a smaller version of the French cathedral in Paris.

Hebrew symbols are inscribed over the front entrance. The myth that has grown up over these emblems is that they signify a "thank you" to the Jewish merchants of Santa Fe who donated money to help in the construction.

According to some, this is a nice but false story. The symbols signify that God or Yahweh is one and the same and that all of humanity are his sons and daughters. Which legend is correct?

Myth or fact? Some Santa Feans claim that Archbishop Lamy is buried under the cathedral. Others say that his crypt at Rosario Cemetery holds his body. Still others declare that the Archbishop is buried out in Lamy. [64]

The Saint Francis Cathedral

SWEET WATER

The Acequia Madre, which means "Mother Ditch," is almost four hundred years old. The Acequia waters the fields and crops of the Canyon Road area. It is the oldest public water utility in the United States. During Spanish Colonial and "Wild West" days, Santa Fe was crisscrossed with acequias that brought water to the different barrios that make up the town. Unfortunately, very little of the old water works is left. What does remain is found in the oldest areas of Santa Fe, as the acequia winds itself through the eastern part of the city. [65]

VIVA MUSIC

Santa Fe's traditional music is known as "Mariachi." The word means the platform in the town square where the musicians play. The word Mariachi has now become a noun that describes a group of musicians who play Mexican music.

Mariachi is a disciplined classical, distinct music that has been in existence for over four hundred and fifty years. Mariachi was born in Mexico but its style was refined in Mexican-American border town parks and cantinas. Mariachi was first introduced to Santa Fe at the La Fonda Hotel in the early 1930s and is now a staple of Santa Fe.

Mariachi is known for its yells, guitar riffs, and serenading lead singer. There is no other music like it in the United States. A Mariachi group can be as small as three players or on up to twenty plus musicians. Mariachi groups dress in flashy Mexican ranchero costumes with big sombreros and Matador-like pants. Like jazz or blue grass music, Mariachi is a unique form of regional music. [66]

FIESTA AND ITS HISTORY

The Santa Fe Fiesta is held on the weekend following the Labor Day holiday. Fiesta celebrates the reconquest of Santa Fe by Diego De Vargas and his Conquistadors in 1692. From Thursday until Sunday, Santa Fe has parades, dances, plays, masses, booths full of food, and gala parties.

In 1680, the Indians revolted and Santa Fe became a battle ground. After a long siege the Spaniards retreated from Santa Fe and New Mexico became a lost province. Twelve years later, an expedition of conquistadors reconquered Santa Fe, and once again Santa Fe was under Spanish rule.

Zozobra, a.k.a. "Old Man Gloom," is a fifty-foot monster effigy made of wire and paper that is burned on the first night of Fiesta. The burning of Zozobra symbolizes the torching of one's thoughts of gloom and worries. Once Zozobra is burnt, Santa Feans are free of troublesome musings and they can revel in the Fiesta celebrations.

The burning of Zozobra takes place at Fort Marcy Park in front of a crowd that comes to watch and be entertained by Mariachi music. Before Zozobra is set on fire, the monster is teased by fire dancers. Finally Zozobra is torched and fireworks explode around the monster's head.

Zozobra's arms flail and its mouth moves by way of cables. The monster's groans are amplified over a sound system as the Fiesta crowd roars at the monster's incineration. The Zozobra legend states that the ghoul is annually captured in a cave in either Pecos or Nambe. The fifty-foot monster is then brought to Santa Fe and burned at the stake. [67]

Zozobra

THE BIG CROSS

The Cross of the Martyrs located atop Fort Marcy Hill was built in 1920. The cross commemorates the twenty-one Franciscan Padres and Monks who were captured by the Indians and then tortured to death during the first days of the Indian Revolt of 1680.

The martyrs were murdered on Fort Marcy Hill because the Indians wanted the besieged Spaniards at the Palace of the Governors to see what would befall them if they did not abandon Santa Fe. Fort Marcy Hill was in plain view of the Palace of the Governors in 1680.

Today the Cross of the Martyrs stands in a tranquil area that includes a beautiful observation deck, and one can see all of Santa Fe below. The walk up to the cross is well worth the effort. Take a camera.

Before there was a Cross of the Martyrs, the hill was home to an American military post. After capturing Santa Fe in 1846, American troops built Fort Marcy, named after William Marcy who was the Secretary of War at that time.

Fort Marcy commanded all of Santa Fe with its cannons. The fort was decommissioned in 1894 and fell into disrepair. Today, if you walk the area around the Cross of the Martyrs you can still see the remains of the earthen redoubts that made up the fortress walls. [68]

THE SANTA FE RIVER

In the 1600s, during Spanish Colonial times, the Santa Fe River was a roaring torrent that had trout in it. The river ran from the mountains that stand behind the Canyon Road area, snaked through Santa Fe, and then emptied into the Rio Grande near La Bajada.

Why is today's Santa Fe River a dried up stream? The answer is dams. The old river channel is blocked by them. The first dam was built in 1881, followed by a replacement for it in 1893. Two other dams were built further up stream in 1926 and 1943.

Consequently, the Santa Fe River has been turned into a dried-up creek. Without the dams Santa Fe would have to deal with the risk of yearly floods.

On the afternoon of July 25, 1968, Santa Fe and the mountains east of town were hit with a three-hour deluge. The water from this cloudburst flooded the arroyos beyond St. John's College and the upper Canyon Road areas.

In a short time, Santa Fe was struck by a flood, the likes of which have never been seen before or since. The Santa Fe River overflowed into the streets and neighborhoods. The river was twelve feet high as measured from channel base to the brim, and some waves on the river reached twenty-four feet in height, from channel base to crest.

Cars, houses, bridges, and trees were swept away. Roads that were built on slopes or in flood basins became streams of mud and debris. Cars that were carried away in the flood waters that hit the Canyon Road areas were later found miles out of town towards the Buckman area. Large parts of Santa Fe were without telephone service or electricity due to the many downed utility lines.

When the three-hour storm ended, Santa Fe and the county were declared a disaster area. It's a good thing, for nobody in Santa Fe had flood insurance. Miraculously, nobody was reported killed during the "Great Flood."

The tallest tale that came out of the '68 flood was the story of a female hobo who was swept away while living under a bridge. The lady managed to climb atop a piece of debris that looked like the top of a piano. The hobo surfed the flood and was never seen again. No doubt a bogus story—every major American flood story has a similar tale of some person shredding the waves on a piece of debris. Tragically, modern Santa Fe is less prepared for a flood than it was in 1968, due to flood plain construction. [69]

The 1968 Flood

THE MOST DANGEROUS ROAD
IN SANTA FE COUNTY

Old State Road 8, according to Santa Fe lore, is known as Suicide Alley. The road runs from Pojoaque to Santa Cruz. The thoroughfare was aptly named. Over the years many fatalities happened on this narrow, scenic, sharp-cornered road.

Many crosses dot the road's apron area; these large crucifixes are known as *descansos*. They mark the place where a loved one died. The cross signifies that the person who passed on no longer has to carry his burdens or cross through this life. The descanso is a unique northern New Mexico, Santa Fe tradition.

Suicide Alley passes through some of the most beautiful country in New Mexico. If you motor down this road, enjoy the sights, buckle up, be aware, and be lucky! [70]

MAD AT JAPAN

In the 1930s, in what is now the Casa Solana neighborhood, bordered by Saint Francis Drive and West Alameda, was a CCC camp (Civil Conservation Corps). The CCC was a Federal program instituted during the Depression of the 1930s.

The men of the CCC were housed and paid by the Federal Government. The CCC men constructed public works or roads around the United States. Santa Fe's Hyde Park lodges and roads were built by the CCC.

During World War II, the Santa Fe CCC camp was used to house American citizens of Japanese ancestry. After Pearl Harbor, Americans of Japanese ancestry who lived on the West Coast were rounded up by the FBI and other Federal forces and forced to live out the war in detainment camps.

The reasoning behind the confinement was that there might be some Japanese spies amongst this group of Japanese-Americans. The internees were fed and clothed and given fairly comfortable quarters.

However, these Americans were denied their constitutional rights, due to prejudice brought on by the sneak attack on Pearl Harbor.

Some of the young American men from the internment camp at Casa Solana joined the army and fought with valor with the 442nd Regimental Combat Team in Italy. The 442nd was made up of Americans of Japanese ancestry. This regiment was the most decorated unit in the Italian Theater.

WORDS TO KNOW

ANDALE: Hurry it up, move it, faster!

ALAMOGORDO: Round or fat cottonwood tree.

ALGODONES: Cotton or cotton fields.

BRUJA: Witch.

CHALE: No way, forget it.

CHAVA: A girlfriend of easy virtue.

CHICANO: A person of Mexican lineage.

CIBOLA: Buffalo.

CUATE: A cousin or a friend.

CUMBRES: A mountain ridge.

ESCONDIDO: Hidden.

FAROLITO: A candle in a sand-based bag, used at Christmas for decorations.

GABACHO: A Spanish term for French soldiers who garrisoned Spain under Napoleon. The occupying Napoleonic soldiers spoke Spanish with a French Gaulic accent. The word gabacho was bastardized in the Southwest and it came to be known as a term that meant white American.

GANAS: With guts and passion.

GRINGO: A light-skinned American. The word is said to have come from the turn of the century American military uniforms that were green. Before that Americans were known as Yanquis or Gabachos. Another version claims the word Gringo comes from a song that was popular with Americans during the 1800s.

GOLONDRINA: Swallow.

HONDO: Deep.

ISLETA: A small isle.

JORNADA DE MUERTO: Journey of death.

KIVA FIREPLACE: The wrong name for today's Santa Fe fireplace. A true kiva fireplace was an area in the middle of a circular room where a fire was burnt. The roof above the fire area had a hole in it so the smoke would escape. Today's Kiva fireplace is in reality a FOGON. The Spaniards introduced the Pueblo Indians to the corner fireplace. A FOGON is made of adobe bricks.

KOKOPELLI: A Kachina doll that is bent over playing the flute while it dances. The symbolism and magic that this Kachina brings is that of happiness and festivities. With the Kokopelli's music, seeds are transformed into crops and maidens conceive children.

KOKO: Zuni Indian Gods, also slang term for some type of entity that is bad and lethal.

LAS VEGAS: The Meadows.

LLANO: A plain.

LOMA: A low hill.

LUMINARIAS: Small bonfires.

MANCANA: It used to mean an Aztec weapon that was the size of a long sword lined with an obsidian edge. Today it means a bat or club.

MIMBRES: A place of willows.

PACHUCO: A man dressed like a zoot-suiter who can either be dashing or hippy-like. This flashy or trampy costume, depending on a person's taste, is worn by guys who used to hang out at dance halls.

PEYOTE: A species of cactus that is a form of reefer that causes hallucinations when it is smoked.

RIATA: Rope or lasso.

SANDIA: Watermelon.

SAPO: A fantastic stroke of luck, be it a shot, a throw of a ball, a roll of a dice, or even a knock-out punch.

SIPAPU: The underworld in certain Indian creation myths.

TIJERAS: Scissors of any size.

TRUCHAS: Trout.

VADO: A ford in the river or lake.

ZACATON: Wild tall grass. [71]

SOURCES

1. Alfred Aragon, *Round The Roundhouse*, October 24, 1996. Mary Lee White, *Santa Fe Reporter*, November 22, 1979. Gussie Fauntleroy, *New Mexican*, October 31, 1999. Antonio R. Garcez, *Adobe Angels: The Ghosts of Santa Fe and Taos*, Red Rabbit Press, 1995. Howard David Passell, *Albuquerque Journal*, May, 29, 1990. Conor L. Sanchez, *New Mexican*, October 31, 2003. La Posada Website.

2. Brother Steve Armenta, *La Herencia Del Norte*, Fall 1997. Alice Bullock, *Santa Fe Reporter*, June 6, 1982. Gussie Faulteroy, *New Mexican*, October 31, 1999. Emily Drabanski, *New Mexican*, October 31, 1982. No author, *New Mexican*, July 13, 1970.

3. Antonio Garcez, *Adobe Angels: The Ghosts of Santa Fe and Taos*, Red Rabbit Press, 1995. Robert Nott, *New Mexican Pasatiempo*, October 24, 2003. Louise Turner, *El Palacio*, Spring 1989.

4. Marc Simmons, *Witchcraft in the Southwest*, University of Nebraska Press, 1980.

5. Scott Beaven, *Albuquerque Journal*, August 9, 10, 11, 12, 1973. Madge Harrar, *Albuquerque Journal Impact Magazine*, August 2, 1983.

6. Emily Drabanski, *New Mexican*, October 31, 1982. Gussie Fauntleroy, *New Mexican*, October 31, 1999. Peter Hertzog, *La Fonda*, Press of the Territory, 1962.

7. Warren A. Beck, *New Mexico: A History of Four Centuries*, University of Oklahoma Press, 1962. Gussie Fauntleroy, *New Mexican*, October 31, 1999. Tim McCurdy, *New Mexico Magazine*, March 1986.

8. "Castle of Spirits," True Ghost Stories Website.

9. Mark Simmons, *Witchcraft in the Southwest*, University of Nebraska Press, 1980.

10. Steve Terrell, *Albuquerque Journal*, February 9, 1985.

11. Alice Bullock, *Living Legends of the Santa Fe Country*, Sunstone Press, 1985. Alice Bullock, *New Mexican*, January 25, 1970. Emily Drabanski, *New Mexican*, October 31, 1982. Gussie Fauntleroy, *New Mexican*, October 31, 1999. Richard McCord, *Santa Fe Reporter*, September 13, 2000.

12. Antonio R. Garcez, *Adobe Angels: The Ghosts of Santa Fe and Taos*, Red Rabbit Press, 1995. All About Ghosts Website.

13. Rosanna Hall, *New Mexican Family Living*, January 9, 1977. Pamela J. Tarchinski, *Albuquerque Journal*, June 14, 1991. Stephen E. Watkins, *Old Santa Fe Today*, University of New Mexico Press, 1982.

14. Bill Brokaw, *Loretto Chapel, the Miraculous Staircase*, The Creative Company, R.L. Ruehrwein Publishers, 2002. Alice Bullock, *Living Legends of the Santa Fe Country*, Sunstone Press, 1985.

15. Stephen DeBorhegi, *El Santuario de Chimayo*, Ancient City Press, 1970. Alice Bullock, *Living Legends of the Santa Fe Country*, Sunstone Press, 1985. Alice Bullock, *New Mexican Pasatiempo*, November 9, 1969. Jacqueline Orsini Dunnington, *Santa Fean*, April 1955.

16. John Brandi, *El Palacio*, Summer 1979. Priscilla O'Connor, Artesia Daily Press, October 12, 1977. Toby Smith, *Albuquerque Journal Impact Magazine*, May 24, 1987.

17. Constant Chapman Private Archive, *Trial of Borrego Brothers*. Lynn Cline, *New Mexican*, October 26, 1997. Wes Gilbreath, *Death on the Gallows: Story of Legal Hangings in New Mexico 1847-1923*, High Lonesome Books, 2003. Aire W. Poldervaart, *Black Robed Justice: A History of the Administration of Justice in New Mexico From American Occupation in 1846 Until Statehood in 1912*, Ayer Company Publications, 1976. Bruno J. Navarro, *New Mexican*, April 2, 1997. Marc Simmons, *Santa Fe Reporter*, January 13, June 30, 1993. Ralph Emerson Twitchel, *Leading Facts of New Mexico History*, Volume II, Torch Press, 1912.

18. Ralph Melnick, *Justice Betrayed: A Double Killing in Santa Fe*, University of New Mexico Press, 2000. Rita Younis, *La Herencia Del Norte*, Spring 1998. No author, *New Mexican*, July 17, 20, 1933.

19. Warren A. Beck, *New Mexico A History of Four Centuries*, University of Oklahoma Press, 1962. Tim McCurdy, *New Mexico Magazine*, March 1986.

20. Pierre Laroche, *New Mexican*, September 26, 1988. Richard McCord, *Santa Fe Reporter*, September 21, 1980. Steve Terrell, *New Mexican*, August 26, 1991. Arnold Vigil, *Albuquerque Journal*, September 27, 1988.

21. No author, *New Mexican*, March 13, 14, 15, 20, 21, 1933.

22. Kevin Easthouse, *New Mexican*, March 29, 1997. Bill Hoffman, Cathy Burke, *Heaven's Gate*, Harper Collins, 1997.

23. Jerome Curry, Loren Coleman, *Fate Magazine*, May 1973. Marc Simmons, *Santa Fe Reporter*, April 17, 1991. No author, *New Mexican*, March 26, 1880.

24. No author, *New Mexican*, March 24, 1933.

25. No author, *New Mexican*, March 7, 1951.

26. No author, *New Mexican*, November 6, 1957.

27. Doyle Akers, *New Mexican,* April 29, 1964. Jerry Smothers, *Albuquerque Journal,* April 29, 1964. No author, *New Mexican,* April 27, 28, 29, 1964. No author, *Albuquerque Tribune,* April 27, 28, 1964.

28. No author, *New Mexican,* March 23, 1970.

29. Zack Van Eyck, *New Mexican,* September 1, 18, 19, 1994. Karl Mofat, *Rio Grande Sun,* September 12, 1996. Andrew Stiny, *Albuquerque Journal,* October 9, 1994. Steve Terrell, *New Mexican,* August 21, 1994.

30. Andrea Buchanan, *Las Vegas Optic,* September 15, 1994. Andrew Stiny, *Albuquerque Journal,* September 20, 1994.

31. Kay Bird, *Santa Fe Reporter,* April 10, 1994. Pavel and Anatoli Sudoplatov, Jerrold and Leona Schecter, *Special Tasks: The Memoirs of an Unwanted Witness—A Soviet Spymaster,* Little, Brown and Company, 1994.

32. No author, *New Mexican,* March 23, 1970.

33. Larry Calloway, *New Mexican,* March 25, 1973. Fray Angelico Chavez, *La Conquistadora,* Sunstone Press, 1975. Ronald Gallegos, *New Mexican,* March 19, April 15, 16, 1973. John Soper, *New Mexican,* June 26, 1973. No author, *New Mexican,* April 29, 1973.

34. Warren A. Beck, *New Mexico A History of Four Centuries,* University of Oklahoma Press, 1962. Thomas E. Chavez, *New Mexican,* October 8, 1990. Marc Simmons, *Santa Fe Reporter,* June 19, 1995. Stephen E. Watkins, *Old Santa Fe Today,* University of New Mexico Press, 1982. Ralph Emerson Twitchel, *The Spanish Archives of New Mexico II,* Torch Press, 1914. Workers of the Writer's Program of the Works Project Administration in the State of New Mexico, *New Mexico Guide to the Colorful State,* Hasting House, 1940.

35. Marc Simmons, *Witchcraft in the Southwest,* University of Nebraska Press, 1980.

36. Warren A. Beck, *New Mexico A History of Four Centuries,* University of Oklahoma Press, 1962. Fern Lyon, *New Mexico Magazine,* February 1983. Marc

Simmons, *Witchcraft in the Southwest*, University of Nebraska Press, 1980. Maurilio E. Vigil, *La Herencia Del Norte*, Summer 1998.

37. Marc Simmons, *Santa Fe Reporter*, June 19, 1995. Ralph Emerson Twitchel, *The Spanish Archives of New Mexico II*, Torch Press, 1914.

38. Stanley Hordes, Boyd Pratt, Cordelia Thomas Snow, David Snow, Linda Tiges, "Santa Fe Historical Plaza Study I & II with Translations From Spanish Colonial Document," City Planning Department, 1990. Ralph Emerson Twitchel, *The Spanish Archives of New Mexico II*, Torch Press, 1914.

39. *Ibid. Ibid.*

40. *Ibid. Ibid.*

41. James A. Crutchfield, *The Santa Fe Trail*, Republic of Texas Press, 1996. David Grant Noble, *Santa Fe, History of an Ancient City*, School of American Research Press, 1989. Don Worchester, *Pioneer Trails West*, Caston Press, 1985.

42. Donald Chuput, *FX Aubry in the Southwest*, A.H. Clark Co., 1975. Marc Simmons, *Ranchers, Ramblers & Renegades*, Ancient City Press, 1984. Marc Simmons, *Yesterday in Santa Fe*, San Marcos Press, 1969. Ralph Emerson Twitchel, *Leading Facts of New Mexico History*, Volume II, Torch Press, 1912.

43. Peter Hertzog, *La Fonda*, Press of the Territory, 1962.

44. Kent Alexander, *Legends of the Old West*, Fairfax Publishing, 1994. Orlan Sawe, *Charles Siringo*, Twayne Publishing, 1981. Marc Simmons, *When Six Guns Ruled*, Ancient City Press, 1990. Dan L. Thrapp, *Encyclopedia of Frontier Biography*, A.H. Clark Co., 1988.

45. George Fitzpatrick, *New Mexico Magazine*, September 1954. Pat Garret, *The Authentic Life of Billy the Kid*, University Oklahoma Press, 1954. Peter Hertzog, *La Fonda*, Press of the Territory, 1962. Robert Kadlec, *They Knew Billy The Kid*, Ancient City Press, 1987. Marc Simmons, *Santa Fe Reporter*, February 14, 1996. Ralph Emerson Twitchel, *Leading Facts of New Mexico History*, Volume II, Torch Press, 1912.

46. Walter Briggs, Howard Bryan, Fray Angelico Chavez, *New Mexico Magazine*, March–April 1971. William W. Davis, *El Gringo, or New Mexico and Her People*, Ayer Company Publishing, April 1973. Maria Higuera, *Albuquerque Journal*, December 8, 1983. April Kopp, *New Mexico Magazine*, October 1991. Beth Morgan, *New Mexican*, January 15, 1984. Marc Simmons, *New Mexico A Bicentennial History*, W.W. Norton & Co., 1977. Marc Simmons, *Santa Fe Reporter*, December 2, 1987; May 15, August 21, 1996. Ralph Emerson Twitchel, *The Occupation of New Mexico, 1846-1851*, Smith Brooks Publishers, 1909.

47. Fern Lyon, *New Mexico Magazine*, February 1983.

48. Wes Gilbreath, "Death on the Gallows," *Story of Legal Hangings in New Mexico, 1847-1923*, High Lonesome Press, 2002. Marc Simmons, *Santa Fe Reporter*, July 31, 1996. Marc Simmons, *When Six Guns Ruled*, Ancient City Press, 1990.

49. Maj. James C. Mokee, *Narrative of the Surrender of a Command of U.S. Forces at Ft. Filmore, New Mexico, July 1861*, Stagecoach Press, 1960. Frances Edward Rogan, *Military History of New Mexico Territory During the Civil War*, University of Utah, 1961. Marc Simmons, *New Mexico A Bicentennial History*, W.W. Norton & Co., 1977. Marc Simmons, *Santa Fe Reporter*, June 5, 1991; June 26, 1996; September 22, 2001. Ralph Emerson Twitchel, *Leading Facts of New Mexico History*, Volume II, Torch Press, 1912.

50. Marc Simmons, *Santa Fe Reporter*, December 22, 1998.

51. Marc Simmons, *Ranchers, Ramblers & Renegades*, Ancient City Press, 1984. Ralph Emerson Twitchel, *Leading Facts of New Mexico History*, Volume II, Torch Press, 1912.

52. *Ibid. Ibid.*

53. Tom Dunlay, *Kit Carson & The Indians*, University of Nebraska Press, 2000. Edgar Hewett, *Kit Carson He Led The Way*, Monographs of the School of American Research, 1946. Frances Edward Rogan, *Military History of New Mexico During the Civil War*, University of Utah, 1961. Edward L. Sabin, Howard Simon, Marc Simmons, *Kit Carson Days 1809-1868: Adventures in the Path of Empire*, University of Nebraska Press, 1995. John Sherman, *Santa Fe A Pictorial History*, Walsworth Publishing, 1984. Stephen E. Watkins, *Old Santa*

Fe Today, University of New Mexico Press, 1982. Marc Simmons, *On the Santa Fe Trail*, University Press of Kansas, 1986. Marc Simmons, *Ranchers, Ramblers & Renegades*, Ancient City Press, 1984. Gerald Thompson, *The Army and the Navajos*, University Press of Arizona, 1976. Ralph Emerson Twitchel, *Leading Facts of New Mexico History*, Volume II, Torch Press, 1912.

54. Alice Bullock, *New Mexican*, September 15, 1974. Wes Gilbreath, *Death on the Gallows: Story of Legal Hangings in New Mexico, 1847-1923*, High Lonesome Press, 2002. Maurice Kildare, *The New Mexico Lawman*, June 1966. The Old Santa Fe Association, *North Side of the Ancient Plaza*, Schifani Brothers Printing Company, 1948. J.W. Schomisch, *New Mexican*, April 26, 1986. Marc Simmons, *Santa Fe Reporter*, January 12, 1994. Monica Soto, *New Mexican*, December 14, 1997. Robert Torrez, *New Mexico Bar Journal*, summer 2000.

55. Fern Lyon, *New Mexico Magazine*, February 1980. James E. and Barbara H. Sherman, *Ghost Towns and Mining Camps of New Mexico*, University of Oklahoma Press, 1975.

56. Peter Hertzog, *La Fonda*, Press of the Territory, 1962.

57. No author, *New Mexican*, July 26, 1974.

58. Ireneo L. Chaves, "New Mexico Historical Review," April 1929. Thomas E. Chavez, *New Mexican*, October 8, 1990. David Grant Noble, *Santa Fe, History of the Ancient City*, School of American Research Press, 1989. Ralph Emerson Twitchel, *Leading Facts of New Mexico History*, Volume I, Torch Press, 1911.

59. Marc Simmons, *Santa Fe Reporter*, May 5, 1993. No author, *New Mexican*, October 15, 1942.

60. Dorsey Griffith, *New Mexican*, April 2, 1989. Oliver LaFarge, *New Mexican*, November 5, 1967. Fern Lyon, *New Mexico Magazine*, February 1983. Marc Simmons, *Santa Fe Reporter*, May 5, 1993. No author, reprint of article, *New Mexican*, November 5, 1967.

61. Tom Day, Peter Katel, *New Mexican*, July 4, 1974. Don Jones, *Albuquerque Journal*, May 7, 1987.

62. Biddle Duke, *New Mexican*, June 21, 1992. Stephen E. Watkins, *Old Santa Fe Today*, University of New Mexico Press, 1982.

63. Stephen E. Watkins, *Old Santa Fe Today*, University of New Mexico Press, 1982.

64. Alice Bullock, *New Mexican Pasatiempo*, July 18, 1971. Stephen E. Watkins, *Old Santa Fe Today*, University of New Mexico Press, 1982.

65. Ruth Chaban, *New Mexican Pasatiempo*, January 3, 1971.

66. Micaela Seidel, *New Mexico Magazine*, May 1994.

67. Gussie Fauntleroy, *New Mexican*, September 12, 1999. Helen Gaussoin, *New Mexico Magazine*, September 1980. David Grant Noble, *History of An Ancient City*, School of American Research Press, 1989. Marta Weigle, Peter White, *The Lore of New Mexico*, University of New Mexico Press, 2003.

68. John Marino, *New Mexican*, January 22, 1993. Jim Neal, *New Mexican*, September 25, 1966. John Sherman, *Santa Fe A Pictorial History*, Walsworth Publishing, 1984. Stephen E. Watkins, *Old Santa Fe Today*, University of New Mexico Press, 1982. No author, *Albuquerque Journal*, June 24, 1954.

69. Ron Longto, Jim Peeler, Chuck Noland, *New Mexican*, July 26, 1968.

70. John Martinez, *New Mexican*, May 11, 1972.

71. Marc Simmons, *Santa Fe Reporter*, October 8, 1984. Workers of the Writer's Program of the Work Project Administration in the State of New Mexico, *New Mexico Guide to the Colorful State*, Hastings House, 1940.

Printed in the United States
20912LVS00003B/268-315